The Earth Is Evil

SERIES EDITORS · *Marco Abel and Roland Végső*

PROVOCATIONS

Something in the world forces us to think.
—Gilles Deleuze

The world provokes thought. Thinking is nothing but the human response to this provocation. Thus, the very nature of thought is to be the product of a provocation. This is why a genuine act of provocation cannot be the empty rhetorical gesture of the contrarian. It must be an experimental response to the historical necessity to act. Unlike the contrarian, we refuse to reduce provocation to a passive noun or a state of being. We believe that real moments of provocation are constituted by a series of actions that are best defined by verbs or even infinitives—verbs in a modality of potentiality, of the promise of action. To provoke is to intervene in the present by invoking an as yet undecided future radically different from what is declared to be possible in the present and, in so doing, to arouse the desire for bringing about change. By publishing short books from multiple disciplinary perspectives that are closer to the genres of the manifesto, the polemical essay, the intervention, and the pamphlet than to traditional scholarly monographs, "Provocations" hopes to serve as a forum for the kind of theoretical experimentation that we consider to be the very essence of thought.

www.provocationsbooks.com

The Earth Is Evil

STEVEN SWARBRICK

UNIVERSITY OF NEBRASKA PRESS · LINCOLN

© 2025 by the Board of Regents of
the University of Nebraska

An earlier version of chapter 4
appeared in *Parapraxis* (2023).

An earlier version of chapter 5 appeared
as "Destituent Ecology" in *Alienocene:
Journal of the First Outernational* (2023).

All rights reserved

The University of Nebraska Press is part
of a land-grant institution with campuses
and programs on the past, present, and
future homelands of the Pawnee, Ponca,
Otoe-Missouria, Omaha, Dakota, Lakota,
Kaw, Cheyenne, and Arapaho Peoples,
as well as those of the relocated Ho-
Chunk, Sac and Fox, and Iowa Peoples.

For customers in the EU with safety/
GPSR concerns, contact:
gpsr@mare-nostrum.co.uk
Mare Nostrum Group BV
Mauritskade 21D
1091 GC Amsterdam
The Netherlands

Library of Congress Control
Number: 2024060642

Set in OFL Sorts Mill Goudy by A. Shahan.
Designed by N. Putens.

Absent thee from felicity awhile.
—*Hamlet*, act 5, scene 2, line 290

CONTENTS

List of Illustrations   *ix*

Provocations   *xi*

Preface   *xiii*

Acknowledgments   *xxi*

1. Outside in the Ecological Machine   1
2. The Earth Is Evil   27
3. Zero-Waste Sex and Other Energy Fictions   53
4. The Lost D   85
5. Libidinal Ecology   107

   Notes   117

ILLUSTRATIONS

1. John Everett Millais, *Ophelia* (1852) 28
2. Still from *Melancholia* (2011) 28
3. Still from *Melancholia* (2011) 31
4. Still from *Melancholia* (2011) 49
5. Still from *Melancholia* (2011) 49
6. Still from *Melancholia* (2011) 51
7. Still from *Night Moves* (2013) 75
8. Still from *Night Moves* (2013) 75
9. Still from *Night Moves* (2013) 78
10. Still from *Night Moves* (2013) 78
11. Still from *Night Moves* (2013) 78
12. Still from *Night Moves* (2013) 81
13. Still from *Night Moves* (2013) 81
14. Still from *Night Moves* (2013) 83
15. Still from *Everything Everywhere All at Once* (2022) 103
16. Still from *It's a Wonderful Life* (1946) 115
17. Still from *It's a Wonderful Life* (1946) 115

PROVOCATIONS

We're fucked.

The four horsemen of the apocalypse—fascism, global capitalism, police terrorism, and technocratic liberalism—have conspired to rob the earth of everything we hold dear. It is time we return the favor. It is time to take back what is rightfully ours: destitution.

Skeptics will say that we have had enough of destitution. Look around; the destitution of the commons is everywhere. But this is a category error. Disaster capitalism is indeed everywhere: in our bodies, our homes, our schools, and our desires. But disaster capitalism cannot dispossess what does not exist. We, friends, are that inexistence. And the powers that be fear it. We fear it.

If, as Jean-Paul Sartre writes, "nothingness lies coiled at the heart of being—like a worm,"[1] and if, according to Jacques Lacan, "desire, a function central to all human experience, is the desire for nothing nameable,"[2] then destitution needs to be on the political agenda.

Let us recite the cynicism of the hour: the Left has lost; the revolution is impossible; critique has run out of steam; there is nothing to do but tinker at the margins of power. We have heard all of this, and we affirm it: *yes*, the planet is in its death throes; *yes*, the capitalist machine has swallowed us whole; *yes*, all the old positions (Marxist, feminist, environmentalist) are exploding; *yes*, the losses are many.

All the better. This is not a callous affirmation. It is a philosophical one. It should be a political one too.

If desire desires nothing nameable, then nothingness is our greatest existential gift. By ceding nothing, we lose everything. By acceding *to* nothing, we break the world. I, for one, would like to see it broken.

Consider the alternatives. Biopower is a baggy conceptual monster at best (we are power; everything is power; no kidding). Rhizome theory is the very stock-in-trade of late-stage capitalism; its flat multiplicity will be the death of us. Deconstruction is liberal discourse par excellence. It promises more and more *to come*, while ensuring nothing changes.[3]

There is undoubtedly much to learn from these regal discourses. Nevertheless, for all the talk of ruination today, we lack the theory that would collectivize loss.

This book is a start in that direction. Welcome to *The Earth Is Evil*. It promises salvage, not salvation; hole-ism, not holism; disquiet, not quiet. Above all, it promises the freedom to enjoy lack.

Join me.

We have nothing to lose but the lack that binds us.

PREFACE

In the months, days, and hours leading up to the 2020 U.S. presidential election, President Donald Trump and his supporters warned that voting would be a debacle. The election would be a sham. We heard that mail-in voting would overwhelm the system. Left-wing extremists would vote twice, thrice! Corpses would cast votes. Worse still, immigrants would have a voice. None of this came to pass. Of course, voter suppression did occur, but the counting of votes went without a hitch. Much to the dismay of the president, who thrived on the spectacle of disorder, voting took place without so much as a bang. It was all whimpers. Until it wasn't.

Incited by a storm of tweets from President Trump's X (formerly Twitter) account urging supporters to "STOP THE COUNT!"[1] mobs of angry, white protestors gathered outside polling centers in predominantly Black communities. They shouted in impassioned discord, "Stop counting!" "Count all the votes!" Different pro-Trump gatherings interpreted their president's commands differently, some taking their directive as a charge to stop the vote, others interpreting it as a charge to count each one. Some protestors split the difference, shouting both messages in schizoid fashion.[2]

Liberals, TV pundits, and the Democratic National Committee were clearer in their messaging: Count all the votes, they demanded. Our democracy depends on it, they argued.

Despite long-standing voter suppression and the racist history of the Electoral College, the Democrats talked about the sanctity of the count. The Republicans, well, they wanted it both ways—to uphold the vote, so long as it worked in their favor.

Outrage at electoral politics is nothing new. What made the 2020 election so eerie, though, especially for leftists, was that the opposition was playing by a familiar script. The Far Right called into question the legitimacy of the vote, the spectacle, and the neoliberal machine. Except, these protestors did not want to abolish the Electoral College due to its racist history and present. They wanted to fix the count, in both senses of the verb. In other words, they wanted to tear down the system to entrench its most authoritarian spokesperson: Trump. Hence Trump's call for a recount. The falsity of his claims aside—claims that the election was rigged, that Antifa had stolen the presidency—he remained embarrassingly committed to making the numbers work. Trump's buffoonery, his bursts of violence, and his sad attempts at staying in power hinged not on suspending the count but on authenticating it. In this regard, resistance from the Democrats was no different. The numbers are in, they said. President-elect Joe Biden won the count (narrowly).

The numbers do not lie, of course. They are exhaustingly self-evident. But something else was at play—is at play—in the politics of accountability.

The 2020 U.S. presidential vote was not a vote for or against white supremacy, police violence, student debt, the climate, or the fate of democracy. All these issues were at play, as they always are, but any sober eye could tell that a vote for Biden was not a vote against the police, anti-Blackness, or extractive capitalism. The 2020 vote was about counting itself, about who gets to be counted. While this may seem like an exceedingly obvious point, I mean more precisely that the demand to count (or discount) every last vote was urged on by both sides to forestall one thing: the uncountable. All involved demanded an exhaustive record. For obvious reasons, the count does matter. The election of Biden signals that most Americans still want to avoid the worst, and I do not for a second wish to say that the math in this case is nugatory.

But it is also true that this particular form of counting has long been superseded by a higher ledger, particularly the interests of Big Data, including algorithmic giants like Google and Amazon. A vote for Biden changes "nothing" (his word)[3] when it comes to these other forms of algorithmic theft and surveillance.[4] How can change come from a system built on prediction and numeric predation?

The demand to count all the votes and get at the "real" will of the people was a red herring. Even after all had been numbered and tallied, the collective vote had already been cast for countability. From the standpoint of capitalism, we are counted whether we choose to be or not. This goes beyond information capitalism; it is rather a philosophical condition of being made visible, and therefore knowable, by the Count—which is not just a vampire puppet but rather a vampire metaphysics. Countability is a properly metaphysical condition in which uncountability has been snuffed out.[5]

When mobs of Trump supporters overtook the Capitol building on the day the election count was to be made official by the Senate (led by the very same Republican senators who had been questioning its legitimacy and fomenting the anger of white nationalists, their counterparts before that day), TV pundits stood aghast. They asked interviewees repeatedly: How could this have happened? In the Middle East, sure; in undemocratic countries, okay. But in America? The thought proved intolerable, or at least the thought was feigned to be. The sad irony for leftists was that the Left had always talked of seizing or demolishing state power for proletariat ends. Meanwhile, on an ordinary day in January, with little more than a conspiracy theory and a presidential Twitter account to light their rebellion, a group of white nationalists took the seat of the U.S. government in a coup attempt. To anyone keeping count, Trump's right-wing mobs enjoyed the full extent of their white privilege by the police, in contrast with Black Lives Matter protesters earlier that year, who were met outside the Capitol with the full spectacle of the U.S. Armed Forces.

On this day, even violent insurrection had been stolen and made a tool of white supremacy. Rebellion against the state apparatus was done in the name of its supreme leader. What is the Left to do when there is no longer a state to smash, when the state not only smashes itself but does so by demanding that its numbers be counted (and recounted)? What is left when both sides, fascists and liberals, can only talk of counting?

What is left to the Left, I argue, is the uncountable.

No doubt, the media was right to call the events of January 6, 2021, intolerable; the fascist coup was intolerable, at least to the majority of Americans who did not vote to reelect Trump. But far more intolerable is the uncountable itself, which by its very nature falls outside of even the most thorough tally. The uncountable is, by definition, ex-cremental (from the Latin *ex-*, "out," and *crēscĕre*, "to grow"), not incremental. It does not add up to an official number.

There are several names for what I call the uncountable in radical theory: the Real of the drives, in Lacanian psychoanalysis; "the part of those who have no part," in Jacques Rancière's antipolice aesthetics;[6] the event in its essential voiding of the status quo, in Alain Badiou's philosophy; Black negativity, as theorized by Frank B. Wilderson III, Saidiya Hartman, Calvin

Warren, and David Marriott.[7] Each of these formulas animates to varying degrees the arguments of this book. However, the main conceptual thread I elaborate here, *with* and *against* the aforementioned discourses, is what I call *destituent ecology*. The destituency does not strive to be counted; indeed, if being counted is the master signifier of constituent politics, Right or Left, then it would be accurate to say that constituent politics—that is, all representational politics—defines itself in opposition to the uncountable remainder that the destituency unpresents.[8]

At its most deflationary, this book argues that there is nothing extraordinary about ecology; it is, to echo Badiou, a banal fact of existence, "free of any *aura*."[9] Yet it is also evidence of a fundamental problem. Ecocriticism is a constituent paradigm; it counts everything (fungi, microorganisms, plants, and animals) in an ever-expanding inclusive network. For all of that, it lacks a theory of rupture or break. That means that questions of "countability" bear on how we construct a properly leftist environmental movement because we have not figured out how to talk about destituency and ecology together. Doing so might help us finally move beyond the impasse of ecocriticism. That means taking "destituent ecology" as a phrase more literally—we need to abandon ecology. Fuck ecocriticism.

The Earth Is Evil calls for an ecology of negativity and draws on the senses of loss, cession, destruction, and escape that inhabit the word "destitution" while remaining fully *within* relation. I call this strange form of relation, after Lacan, the nonrelation, and I use it to leverage distance from the demands of environmentalism's big Other (the social-symbolic codes that define material life).

The reigning ideology of ecocriticism can be summed up in a well-known phrase by the novelist E. M. Forster: "Only connect!"[10] Interconnection is the buzzword of ecocriticism, as are terms like entanglement and mesh. From massive hyperobjects to actor-networks and rhizomatic agencies, ecocriticism is enthralled by metaphors of interconnection. The reason is simple. Interconnection offers an alternative to the top-down models of psychoanalysis, Marxism, and other forms of ideology critique. The problem with this ecological refrain, "Only connect," is that it is fully of a piece with capitalist logic. We are never more enmeshed in capitalist thinking than when we believe ourselves to be one with the web of life. To say the least, it is troubling that this logic has become the doxa of environmental theory. Although there is, I maintain, still much to learn from the likes of Gilles Deleuze and Félix Guattari, their polemic against psychoanalysis, exemplified in the statement, "We are tired of trees," has lost much of its punch.[11] Worse still, the rejection of verticality in favor of flat, rhizomatic flows has been co-opted. The rhizome is everywhere: in the Amazon warehouse, corporate workplace, and university. Theory at large has become a vehicle for this "saturated immanence," offering hyperconnection at the expense of radical critique.[12]

The Earth Is Evil leverages the Lacanian formula on sexuality, "There's no such thing as a sexual relationship," to open new conceptual space in environmental politics and theory.[13] My claim is that ecotheory makes it difficult, if not impossible, to think outside the network of objects and relations. While this immanentism was useful for overturning the big divides between subject and object and nature and culture—divisions that pervaded theory before the likes of Bruno Latour, Karen Barad, and Jacques Derrida's late work on animality—the focus on immanence in ecological theory has become stifling. Terms like "rhizome," "assemblage," and "actor-network" are used across the theoretical spectrum as answers to a wide range of problems, from human exceptionalism to multispecies ethics to environmental toxicity. Although terms like "assemblage" revived theory, they have become tired—indeed, restrictive.

The biggest problem that ecological theory now faces isn't the divide between nature and culture but the divide between its own immanentism and what I call the *destituent act*.

The latter entails a form of self-destitution pertaining to the subject's libidinal attachment to loss. Freud calls this libidinal attachment the death drive. Lacan calls it the nonrelation. In both cases, destitution involves a relation to the outside—to what transcends the network of objects and relations, including self-relations: the uncountable dimension in us all.[14] *The Earth Is Evil* theorizes the nonrelation in opposition to the reigning theories of ecological entanglement and does so by foregrounding psychoanalysis in the critique of extractive capitalism.

ACKNOWLEDGMENTS

I want to thank Marco Abel and Roland Végső for welcoming this book into the Provocations series. Marco and Roland have created an inspiring home for theory, and I am grateful to be a part of it.

Thanks to Courtney Ochsner at the University of Nebraska Press, with whom it was a pleasure to work; my two anonymous readers for their erudite reports; and Matthew John Phillips, whose meticulous scrutiny of this book helped save me from excess embarrassment.

I owe a debt of gratitude for the friendship of Jean-Thomas Tremblay, who still talks to me even after I recommended *Avatar: The Way of Water*.

I appreciate the support of Timothy Aubry, Eugenie Brinkema, Sam Creely, Drew Daniel, Jessie Hock, Leigh Claire La Berge, Frédéric Neyrat, Benjamin Parris, Mario Telò, and Elizabeth A. Wilson—stellar colleagues and trusted friends.

My thanks to Michelle Rada, Hannah Zeavin, and Frédéric Neyrat for their editorial guidance.

Finally, I thank Rebecca van Laer, who has heard me talk about symbolic castration more than anyone should have to endure. This book is for her.

The Earth Is Evil

1

Outside in the Ecological Machine

Let us begin with the problem.

While Marxism has found an ally in environmental movements and Freudo-Marxism still lives on sporadically, there is no *psychoanalytic* ecocriticism that foregrounds Freud's theory of the unconscious.[1] One reason why psychoanalysis is not included in ecotheoretical discussions can be found in the poet H.D.'s *Tribute to Freud*, a memoir recounting her experience undergoing psychoanalytic treatment. H.D. recalls one of Freud's more worrying statements: "One day he said, '*Today we have tunneled very deep.*' One day he said, 'I struck oil. It was I who struck oil. But the contents of the oil wells have only just been sampled. There is oil enough, material enough for research and exploitation, to last fifty years, to last one hundred years—or longer.' He said, 'My discoveries are not primarily a heal-all. My discoveries are a basis for a very grave philosophy.'"[2] Freud's metaphor, comparing the unconscious to subterranean oil wells, isn't helping the psychoanalytic case. The metaphor smacks of the very sort of extractive "research and exploitation" of fossil fuels that has unleashed, in our present age of anthropogenic climate change, environmental conditions so unthinkable that they rival the most surreal psychoanalytic dream scenarios—a sixth mass extinction that makes the death drive look quaint. Freud was, of course, a believer in the importance of dreams. But the capitalist dream reforming our planet and making life unlivable for billions of humans and nonhuman species echoes the very same metaphor of untapped oil in which Freud indulges. The fantasy of reaching the oily depths of the unconscious hits on an existential danger: that the object of psychoanalysis (repressed sexuality) and the object of capitalism (pressurized materiality, i.e., "oil") are the same. Psychoanalysis and fossil capitalism would appear to be caught in the same destructive loop. The depth model of the former echoes the extractive model of the latter. Freud admits, "My discoveries are not primarily a heal-all." Even so, his metaphor of extracting oil for future exploitation is not only bad environmentalism, to use Nicole Seymour's phrase,[3] but also bad psychoanalysis. It is strangely *un*-Freudian.

The Freudian theory of the unconscious, especially in its Lacanian reformulation, is, contrary to Freud's metaphor, not a theory of accumulation at all. It is a theory of loss. Psychoanalysis, unlike any other social theory, posits loss as the true object of our enjoyment. This object or nonobject is a mercurial one, garnering comparisons to a shape-shifting alien.[4] The truth is that desire takes on this horrifying aspect because it only exists as loss. Desire doesn't seek a complementary object, as heterosexism posits. What it seeks is a unique kind of nothing-object, and this encounter with nothing haunts the ecological subject with a traumatic, unconscious remainder. Far worse than oil spills or carbon emissions, desire is, in this unconscious regard, terrifying to the subject of ecocriticism, because it splits the subject in two. Although Freud claims that human desire aims at refinding the lost object, what it really finds through the detours of human longing isn't the primordial thing but the loss—or nothing—that triggers desire in the first place.[5] Loss is consequently a vexing kind of thing. Though we fill out loss through fantasy, the objects of fantasy inevitably turn up empty. The reason, Freud argues, is that loss is there from the start. Loss doesn't just happen to us. It isn't simply the effect of an external cause. Freud, in contradistinction to the entire philosophical tradition, makes loss a strange kind of cause. Loss, in Freud's theory, *causes* the thing. Not only that, loss causes the subject to desire the thing, which, it turns out, is no-thing at all. Throw Freudian causality into the mix, and the whole ontological tradition explodes.

Ecocriticism has been slow to reckon with this explosion. While Marxist ecocriticism can explain in scintillating detail the mechanisms of immiseration and alienation affecting the "web of life,"[6] the goal of such a reading is invariably to lift alienation—to overcome loss and restore the web of life. Psychoanalysis cannot provide this act of restoration. For the cutting edge of psychoanalysis—what makes psychoanalysis something other than a web—is its insistence on the inextricability of loss from desiring subjectivity. As subjects of the unconscious, we are driven to repeat loss again and again. Freud's insight isn't the popularized version of psychoanalysis, that we suffer from a lack of x. The true breakthrough of Freudian psychoanalysis is that we suffer, repeating loss, because we unconsciously *enjoy* the lack of x. Striking oil is, from this psychoanalytic perspective, a perfect example of how consciously we misrecognize the true object of our enjoyment. Although Freud fantasizes about obtaining underground riches, his own theory militates against that fantasy. At the level of the unconscious, not striking oil is the way to enjoyment. Freud's great insight isn't the spatially driven one that, beneath the surface of consciousness, a well of underground contents lies in wait. Freud's insight is that desire is inherently discontented. The Freudian unconscious isn't so much a hyperobject, though it is spatially and temporally complex—a thing we bump up against daily. The unconscious is primarily a hypo-object, or nothing-object; it environs a void.

When satisfaction is linked to loss, as psychoanalysis argues, no amount of vital matter can fill the void left by the unconscious. Freud himself tries to fill that void with images of petroleum.[7] But filling the loss that Freud associates with desire is not only foolhardy, because loss is there from the start, but it is also destructive. Freud's and later Lacan's great fear was that the fantasy of fulfillment would override the subject's true basis in loss. It is not hard to see why. Loss carries with it the tenor of inevitable dissatisfaction. Furthermore, a "grave philosophy" built on loss is not likely to gain many followers. The current absence of ecopsychoanalysis, coupled with the recent turns in literary theory away from psychoanalysis to surface, affective, and reparative reading models, evidences this point. What these models all have in common is the following: to be done with Freud. The desire to chuck Freud to the wastebin of history is an unfailing feature of postcritique; it is downright Oedipal. Nonetheless, Freud and Lacan maintained that orienting ourselves to loss, a loss installed by the symbolic order, is—if not a "heal-all"—a way to prevent the worst. Today, the worst-case scenarios of climate change get worse by the hour. My contention is that the true value of psychoanalysis is not what Freud metaphorized as oil—that is, an exploitable depth. The value that psychoanalysis adds to ecological theory is a negative one. Unconscious desire, as Freud theorized it, has no object.

Because of the privilege psychoanalysis gives to the alienating role of signification, ecocriticism has largely shied away from psychoanalysis in favor of a broad spectrum of vital objects, untamed affects, and ecological entanglements, all promising to fill the gaps left by the Freudian unconscious. Even an ecocriticism that uses the idiom of "unconscious" frequently does so in an altogether unknowing way to mean subconscious or preconscious.[8] Gone from this discourse is the split subject of desire, for whom every object is a source of discontent. In place of the split subject, ecocriticism offers a nonalienated subject fully attuned to its environment. Although ecocriticism believes that it rebels against psychoanalytic oil, it ultimately repeats it. Like Freud's metaphor, ecocriticism is purely content driven, because it disregards the primacy of our alienation. It thinks of subjectivity as a whole—when, really, it is a hole.

I propose a different reading of Freud's metaphor. Against the manifest content of a newly discovered "cheap nature,"[9] Freud's metaphor breaks in on itself, interrupting, like a slip of the tongue, the satisfaction that the image of psychoanalytic oil represents. Freud's metaphor, read in light of Freud's own theory of the unconscious, introduces the very thing that desire desires most: failure. Even if Freud were to arrive at buried contents, by his own theory, any such content would leave a remainder—a hole. Lacan calls this remainder *objet a*, emphasizing the radical otherness of desire to itself. Following Freud, Lacan stresses that the lost object of desire acts as a vortex, causing the subject to desire while that lost object itself remains unobtainable. Striking oil is, in this sense, an elaborate and costly detour toward getting what we truly want: loss itself. Consequently, those who succeed the most at accumulating a lot of things are, according to Lacan, the biggest losers; they have not yet succeeded at enjoying loss.

If psychoanalysis has seemed like a losing effort, unserviceable to the demands of reparative reading, this is because psychoanalysis has not been sufficiently understood as a radical theory of divestment. The Freudian theory of the unconscious has this and only this to say to the capitalist subject: divest! A psychoanalytic ecology geared toward loss has zero interest in accumulating a lot of things. By training subjects to divest from their fantasied objects, which are almost always energy-intensive objects, psychoanalysis teaches capitalist subjects to leave fossil fuels (oil, gas, and coal) in the ground.

The short-circuiting of desire's destructive detour is the biggest stumbling block that psychoanalysis poses to ecocriticism. Though the politics of divestment certainly accords with mainstream ecocritical objectives, the unconscious drive to divest from accumulation also entails divesting from the fantasy of ecological wholeness. The fantasy of the whole reigns supreme in ecocritical discourse. It is the underwriting logic of every reparative reading. Even the most thoroughly deconstructed subject finds herself entangled—the seemingly endless sprawl of deconstructed particulars sutured in the end. But this aspirational entanglement is inherently contradictory. The ecological subject mirrors point for point the aspirational ideology of capitalism, which promises to make desiring subjects whole. The most eco-utopian futures are, consequently, repetitions of the capitalist order. Worse, they perpetuate that order by repressing the split subject of desire.

By contrast, the split subject in psychoanalysis is inexorable. It is not an accidental split foisted on us by external forces. Rather, the split between drive, which has no object and is contentless, and fantasy, which fills in the drive with so many contents, *is* the very unfoundation of thought, including ecological thought. Although Freud forgets this point when turning to psychoanalytic oil, forgetting is, according to his own theory, one of the ways the unconscious drive satisfies itself by re-creating an absence where there would otherwise be a memory. Freud's failure to apply his theory is a clear example of psychoanalytic theory in action.

Giving What We Don't Have

Because the drive has no object besides loss, it not only spoils the fantasy of obtaining a wholly satisfying object, whether a person or thing, but also *enjoys* the process of losing. The drive enjoys at our expense. Lacan furthers Freud's argument about the destituting force of the drive and shows how human beings subjected to the law of signification break *into* desire by breaking *off* pieces of their own most prized bodily possessions.

Already in "Negation," Freud had speculated that "the antithesis between subjective and objective does not exist from the first";[10] the infant exists in a world of autoeroticism without division. The subject–object antithesis must, therefore, be *produced*. Through weaning, the infant not only separates from its caretaker but also learns to "*refind*" its objects, including its most precious object, the ego, against a backdrop of loss.[11] The presence and absence of the breast, the incomplete demands of the Other, all memorably captured by Freud in his recollection of his grandson, who uses the signifiers "fort" (gone) and "da" (there) to make sense of the gaps and vivisections in his newly divided world, slowly constitute the subject as a *subject of loss*.

Lacan's *Anxiety* seminar furthers Freud's argument by adding a surprise twist. It is not just that the subject emerges against a background of loss. According to Lacan, the subject, to *become* a subject, sacrifices or cedes parts of its body to the Other. Like a lizard, salamander, starfish, or lobster, the infant destitutes (abandons, destroys) parts of itself to escape the perilous demands of the Other. These ceded objects become the libidinized objects of the child's (and later the adult's) world. Desire is, in this Lacanian sense, an empty circuit. Although desire opens up to the world, it does not open out to the world. On the contrary, the orifices of the bodily drives take in the world only to empty it (to destitute it).

The difficulty of Lacan's lesson is that the lost or ceded objects (what Lacan calls *objet a*) only exist retroactively *as lost*. The lost object is, therefore, the object par excellence of *Nachträglichkeit*, or retroaction. By ceding the lost object to the Other, the subject is free to fantasize about that loss. Put differently, the subject loses the object *into* being by way of fantasy. Through the loss of this special object, *objet a*, the subject becomes a desiring subject for the first time. It gains a foothold on desire outside the Other and a minimal consistency through fantasy. The way it maintains this minimal consistency is by repeating the loss, the foundational act of cession, that inaugurated desire in the first place. The child plays at throwing its object away, but not to get it back. On the contrary, the child throws the object away to maintain the distance required for the fantasy of retrieval. What is retrieved, ultimately, is never the thing, but the fragment of the "Thing," miniaturized as little *objet a*, which is both integral to the subject and grotesque, a reminder of its own (and the Other's) incognizable jouissance. It is to escape "the thing in me more than me" that I throw a piece of myself away. Desire is born from the discard.

The lost object has no substance prior to being lost, which is why the substance of the libido is essentially mutational, monstrous, shape-shifting, and alien, because it is informed by a formless nothing. Hence, any effort to "*refind*" the lost object is ultimately impossible. The subject of desire can only repeat the loss or sacrifice—the first act of cession—that instituted desire in the first place. Simply put, I lose my desired objects so that I can pursue them; the most coveted objects are thus the ones that incarnate and sustain loss (for example, a lover's inscrutable gaze, an art object that has a certain *je ne sais quoi*). Destitution is always split—we institute objects of desire (the new job, the new car, the new fantasy *x*) so that we can lose them (again).

Anxiety emerges primordially when desire has no exit— that is, *not* when the object is missing (as Freud thought) but when the object is too *present*.[12] Lacan writes, "Anxiety isn't about the loss of the object, but its presence. The objects aren't missing."[13] The foundational act of desire, according to Lacan, is sacrifice. The subject destroys or cedes parts of itself (parts that will later become the phantom objects of desire—the breast, voice, feces, gaze, and so on) in the very act of becoming a subject of desire. We are, in this sense, the direct result of the *disjecta membra* we abandon or flee. Paradoxically, we, as desiring subjects, escape (into) ourselves. Lacan compares this repetitive process of detachment (repetitive because the act of self-sacrifice happens not once but for all time—anytime, for example, we fantasize about the lost object, we lose that object again) to an act of cession:

> In the main, it's not true that the child is weaned. He weans *himself*. He detaches himself from the breast, he plays. After the first experience of cession, ... he plays at detaching himself from the breast and taking it up again. If there weren't already present something active enough for us to be able to articulate it in the sense of a desire for weaning, how could we even conceive of the very primitive facts, which are quite primordial in their appearance, of the refusal of the breast, the first forms of anorexia whose correlations at the level of the Other our experience teaches us to seek out right away?[14]

What is remarkable about Lacan's theory is that it interweaves two seemingly contradictory processes: loss, on the one hand, and refusal, on the other. The first form of freedom, Lacan argues, is anorexia, or the desire for an empty mouth. "[The child] weans *himself*"—that is, destitutes himself (the breast, feces, voice, and gaze all being part of the child's originally enveloped world)—so that desire can break free.

Self-division may sound like a close version of ecological entanglement—particularly Karen Barad's influential formula, "relata do not preexist relations."[15] This idea holds that there are no given entities but rather intra-active agencies. "Agential realism" (Barad's term) refers to quantum entanglement; it is nearly impossible to imagine because, in it, there is quite literally no-thing, no stable entity or object. The subject–object poles of existence only come into being through what Barad calls "agential cuts." Whereas Lacan says that only language cuts and gives shape to reality, Barad argues that matter is already self-cutting; in other words, material reality cuts into itself, self-organizes, and creates boundaries within matter. Matter, or nature, does not require an agential cut from the outside—that is, language or the signifier. Barad claims that nature is both primary process and secondary process at once. Because matter is agential, it is both the product and the agent of cutting; therefore, the apparatuses of cutting are infinite. What Lacan calls symptom, the intrusion of the Real into the symbolic order, Barad calls intra-action, the intrusion of all things into everything else.

Lacan flirts with ecological metaphors, including insect anatomy and viviparous births, to underscore the divisions that constitute the split subject of the unconscious. But ecological entanglement, his theory is not. For what the ecological soup of interrelated parts cannot think, or tolerate for that matter, is an agency that *loses itself into being*. The ecological formula (i.e., *relations precede the relata*) psychoanalytically revised would be *nonrelations precede the relata*. To be sure, there are relations, relations upon relations that are biological, chemical, affective, and so on. But for there to be a subject in the strict sense, a desiring subject, something must fall *out*. The nonrelation is, in psychoanalysis, the uncountable remainder that ecotheory tries but fails to quilt together through metaphors of entanglement. This quilting is impossible because the lost object of desire never really existed to begin with. It was never part of an ecological network; the lost object of desire *incurves* that network.

The lost or ceded object has no substance and, therefore, no possible ontological relation prior to being lost. It only comes into being in and through loss, retroactively through the fantasy of its obtainment. Ecocriticism cannot tolerate this residue of loss. It cannot tolerate the nonobject, or nothing-object, that psychoanalysis makes primary to relationality as such, because to do so would be to admit an obtrusive outside *in* the quilt work of our ecological relations.[16] The Lacanian perspective is not that these biological, chemical, geological, atmospheric, and technological relations do not exist; their existence is plain to see. The psychoanalytic point is that these relations quilt an unknowable remainder. All life, then, would have to be construed as a symptom of the uncountable remainder that Lacan calls lack. Though lack has a bad reputation—indeed, all life and the quilt work of our ecological relations tries to cover over the lack of a generalized castration—from another angle, lack is wildly fecund. To cede is, after all, the flip side of seeding. Loss, psychoanalytically speaking, seeds an unknowable future. This perhaps is why Lacan calls the unconscious the *"unborn."*[17] Through the repetition of lack, life continues to generate itself contradictorily as *negative life*.[18]

Nothing at the Bottom of Everything

The ceded object is an impossible object, birthed into (non) existence through the same retroactive process that births and subsequently haunts the subject—the subject being the excremental aftereffect of cession. Neither the ceded object nor the remaindered subject has a place in the entangled network of ecological relations. Instead, they *divest* from relation, refusing it, spitting it up. This may sound like a recipe for destruction. It is and is not. Although the child ex-ists by expelling parts of its body (parts that were never really theirs to begin with), this inaugural act of destruction braids a desire for the object to return. In refusing the ceded object, the subject *accedes* to a desire for the future—a desire for what will, in the chain of objects to come, masquerade in the place of the lost object. If destitution only named an act of destruction, destituent ecology would be a redundant concept at best. The destruction of all things by liberal deregulation, ecocidal capitalism, TERF warfare, cis heteronormativity, and white supremacy does not need such a theory. But these forms of destructivity can never accede to loss. Capitalism is the clearest example. A capitalist system driven to maximize profit will unleash endless devastation and impoverish the planet, but it cannot accede to loss as such. Once loss becomes the object of desire, as it is for Lacan's destituent subject, capitalist accumulation can no longer function. Although loss is a byproduct of capitalism and fuels a whole range of consumerist fantasies (as the TV series *Mad Men* brilliantly depicts),[19] capitalism cannot make cession its goal.[20] The same is true of ecocriticism. Because ecotheory fashions itself as a constituency of interlocking parts, it repeats capitalist ideology even when it claims to be undermining it. It cannot imagine a constitutive loss, as psychoanalysis does. Instead of ceding its way toward desiring subjectivity, ecologism *cedes its desire*; it makes the lack of lack (anxiety) synonymous with life as such.

The Earth Is Evil, by contrast, maintains that we cede too much to ecological holism when we imagine ourselves as part of the web of life. Refusing to cede on its desire—refusing, too, to cede more than what has already been stolen by the mechanisms of police brutality, neoliberal abandonment, ecocidal destruction, endless detention, ICE, and the full powers of white supremacy—the destituent ecology I theorize never stops writing itself *in* and *out* of existence.

By destituent ecology, I mean something close to what environmental philosopher Frédéric Neyrat calls "renunciation." "To renounce" the earth, Neyrat writes, "means to abandon (the use, the enjoyment of something), to undergo abnegation, but also to *announce a return (re-nuntiare)*, thanks to a kind of *backward movement* suggested by the prefix (*re-*). In this sense, renunciation is a form of *resilience through separation*: to undo, to withdraw, but in order to, in the end, announce or propose another vision of the world."[21] Separation, according to Neyrat, affirms our ecological relations and, for that reason, rejects, along with the new materialisms, any facile notion of a split between nature and culture. However, unlike the now not-so-new materialisms, in which the "relation" is all there is, separation leaves room for what in nature, as in us, is *more than us*. This something more takes on many different names, depending on the philosopher in question: "traject" (Neyrat), "excess" (Bataille), "anti-production" (Deleuze and Guattari), "Real" (Lacan). But its main defining feature is that it loosens our hold on the earth.

It is entirely conceivable, Neyrat argues, to separate *from* while remaining fully attached *to* the earth—to destitute, as Lacan and Slavoj Žižek put it.[22] In a powerful reading of the speculative fiction of W. E. B. Du Bois, Saidiya Hartman posits that, in a world territorialized by white supremacy, Black life becomes possible only in the aftermath of the world, after a cataclysmic separation. "Environmental catastrophe produces this sweeping transformation," Hartman writes. "The paradox is that human extinction provides the answer and the corrective to the modern project of whiteness, which Du Bois defines as *the ownership of the earth forever and ever*, the possessive claim of the universe itself."[23] "In the wake of the disaster, ... the last black man on earth," concludes Hartman, "will be permitted to live as a human for the first time. ... He is alive because the world is dead."[24]

Hartman's reading of environmental catastrophe works in parallax, knowing full well that Du Bois's speculative account means that the reverse is also true, that insofar as the world is alive and insofar as white supremacy remains in possession of "*the earth forever and ever*," Black life will remain in death's position.[25] To renounce the earth is to take up cause with this deathly position, the "sweeping transformation" that, at least in Du Bois's fiction, is represented by environmental catastrophe.

Ecotheory cannot perform this act of renunciation. Caught within its own web of interrelated life, ecotheory neglects what makes life desirable in the first place—not the profusion of animate objects, each one melting into the next, but the lack that comes with the subject's inaugural act of cession and destruction. To destroy, in this sense, is not punk refusal. The problem of refusal for refusal's sake has been rightly critiqued by Marxist critics Jodi Dean and Anna Kornbluh. Dean (with Kai Heron) criticizes various anarcho-environmentalist groups for romanticizing "disaster communism";[26] meanwhile, Kornbluh upbraids postcritique for imperiling the ecology of "big ideas" in favor of weak theories tuned to the pitch of capitalist dissolutionism. Kornbluh singles out destitution, especially in its Agambenian and Latourian variants, as a key culprit in the undermining of the political imagination:

> Dissolution and dismantling are celebrated as the opposite of constituting; the phenomenally popular philosopher Giorgio Agamben names this value "destituency" (from the Latin *de + statuere*—to move away from setting things up, deserting, forsaking, abandoning). Constituting is violent containment; destituting is lavish unforming. Our eminent theorists thus proclaim themselves "unbuilders," equating building with dubious synthesis and the made form. Formlessness as aesthetic value animates anarchy as ethico-politico value—but the question of critique in the time of extinction requires that at least we hear how the vitalist mantra "burn it all down" rhymes rather much with the institutional embers on our incinerating planet.[27]

This is scintillating critique. But it overrides the contradiction of dialectical thought and the paradox of negativity. Dialectic does not mean that constitution and destitution are antithetical (although Kornbluh is undoubtedly an expert dialectician, she, like Marx, "a positive dude," gives construction the win at the end of the day). Instead, dialectic means that constitution and destitution are intertwined—one divides (cuts into) the other.[28] This is to say, I agree wholeheartedly with Kornbluh. Up with big ideas! Down with postcritique! And yet the *de-* I foreground here emanates from the same structures that Kornbluh seeks to preserve.

Oddly, Kornbluh's critique of Latourian horizontality, an adjunct to the dissolutionism she upbraids, ends up repeating Latour's call to stop deconstructing and start building, making, and aligning. Both Kornbluh and Latour echo Joe Biden's alliterative slogan, "Build Back Better." Talk about the material ecology of ideas! But building back better misses the paradox of dialectics—the institution becomes a corrective to extinct critique in Kornbluh's argument. My point is that this corrective overcorrects; it forgets the undercorrection or undermining that any positive institution entails. After all, the ceded object theorized by Lacan splits in two directions: toward the lost object, which haunts subjectivity with its uncountable remainder, and toward the institution of the subject, who becomes a desiring subject in and through a primordial sacrifice. Lacan's theory of destitution is, therefore, contradictory in the sense that it maintains the necessity of the desiring subject while also showing that desiring subjectivity is inherently lacking.

This commitment to contradiction, exemplified by the Lacanian insistence on the drive in contradistinction to conscious pleasure or need, puts him at odds with the main current of "destituent power" coming from Martin Heidegger (whose philosophy proposes nothing less than the destruction of the Cartesian subject and the clearing of metaphysics), as well as from Michel Foucault, Giorgio Agamben, and the anarchist collective Tiqqun, who likewise assert that all organized structures are vehicles of power (Foucault), akin to the concentration camp (Agamben), and needing dismantling in favor of nonhierarchical, rhizomatic flows (Tiqqun). Then there's Deleuze and Guattari, who (following Louis Althusser's theory of interpellation) summarize the destituent thesis on subjectivity in the following: "There is no subject, only collective assemblages of enunciation. Subjectification is simply one such assemblage and designates a formalization of expression or a regime of signs rather than a condition internal to language. . . . Capital is a point of subjectification par excellence," suggesting that "the psychoanalytic cogito" is another.[29] For these thinkers, subjectivity is a trap, because it seems to put a stop to Dasein's endless questioning (Heidegger), life's creative evolution (Deleuze), and bodies and their pleasures (Foucault). Yet the theorist who most comes to mind when thinking about destitution is, arguably, Jacques Derrida, whose philosophy begins by critiquing the phenomenology of presence and ends in an endless state of mourning for that which is, according to Derrida, always already lost. Derrida's dogged interrogation of contradictions, such as mourning that which never really existed, highlights how close deconstruction is to the destituent ecology I derive from Freud and Lacan. It also signals their radical divergence.

No Thing

Derrida is a radical Kantian. Whereas Kant bars the thing-in-itself and says, essentially, that there is something beyond knowledge but we cannot know it outside our formal ways of thinking (our frames of reference forbid access to the thing-in-itself), Derrida takes up the Kantian excision of the thing to say that not only can we not access things in the raw but also there has never been and will never be the thing-in-itself.[30] The thing is an illusion of the metaphysics of presence. In other words, the thing-in-itself and all its many avatars are effects of our forms of knowing, our frames of reference. Moreover, these forms of knowing are not permanent, as Kant believed, but are themselves mutable and forever sliding. So not only is the thing, anchor of being, illusory, but the very means by which we can know and access the thing are also indeterminate. This is Derrida's Saussurean critique of phenomenology, which he extends in his analysis of Husserl and Heidegger and countless others who he claims fall victim to the metaphysics of presence.[31] Saussure famously argues that, in language, there are no positivities. Language, composed of signifiers, is a system of negativity without presence. The whole Derridean apparatus repeats this insight with and against thinkers like Kant, Saussure, and Heidegger, who, he argues, limit the play of signification. Derrida's project is to unleash the signifier's unlimited negativity and to banish the vestiges of presence haunting Kant (thing-in-itself), Saussure (synchronic system of meaning), and Heidegger (withdrawn presence of Being).

However, Derrida does not completely escape the trap he argues others fall victim to. Derrida recognizes, rightly, that the metaphysics of presence, however conceived, assigns meaning retroactively to that which is always already absent. Thus, hauntology, for Derrida, doesn't refer to the ghosts of once living, now extinct, beings. Hauntology is the retroactive illusion of lost presence. Kant, for example, is retroactively haunted by the thing-in-itself, just as Heidegger is retroactively haunted by the forgetting of Being. Derrida takes from Freud the latter's insight about retroactivity, that the future changes the past. We typically think of the past as fixed and determined and the future as radically open. Derrida, following Freud, argues that the past and future are open because the future, which is contingent, is always rewriting the past, assigning meaning to a signifying chain that is always sliding.

Derrida bemoans this retroactive loop and the problem it raises, which is that we can never escape the metaphysics of presence entirely. The history of philosophy is proof that we are indeed trapped. Kant could not shake free of the idea of the thing. Heidegger, likewise, holds on to the presence of Being even in its absence as dis-closure. And Lacan, Derrida claims, remains a phallocentric thinker, believing in the lost phallus.

Derrida's project can thus be described as an endless performance of melancholia, mourning that which never really existed and caught in the loop of absence and presence. It is an interminable project that makes action impossible. Hence his predilection for Hamlet. His critique of Hegel illustrates this point.

Hegel begins the *Phenomenology of Spirit* stating that the preface is impossible. The beginning only acquires meaning by reaching the Absolute, or the ending, Hegel's version of *Nachträglichkeit*. In other words, meaning happens retroactively in Hegel's philosophy. Derrida agrees. The supplement (difference) is precisely retroactivity at work. Yet, for Derrida, the supplement works by undermining what came before it, proving, finally, that language is always sliding, disjoined from the symbolic. Thus, Derrida's critique of Hegel is that Hegel is not Hegelian enough. Hegel states that the preface is impossible and then *writes the preface*. Would it not be better, deconstructively speaking, to forego the preface—to reduce it to the play of difference? Here, though, is the Hegelian gambit—the preface *is* impossible, all the better. Hegel doesn't disseminate the preface; instead, he embraces the contradiction, writing what cannot be written. In short, Hegel affirms the impossible act.

In "Form and Meaning," Derrida displaces the contradictory act, the only act possible in the views of Hegel and Lacan, into the "ellipsis" of form. "This displacement," Derrida confesses, "is no doubt deficient, but with a deficiency that is not yet, or is already no longer, absence, negativity, nonbeing, lack, silence."[32] These terms, "absence, negativity, nonbeing, lack, silence," are too stationary and so fail to pass the test of deconstruction.

Here, Lacan could not be more different. He admits that the presence of the One, or the phallus, is an illusion propagated by retroaction. Nevertheless, he maintains that the illusion isn't lamentable because that very illusion enables subjects to desire in the first place. Thus, he agrees with Derrida—there is no stable referent outside of signification. However, with respect to Kant, he concedes that there is *something* beyond the play of the signifier, something hard and fixed: the *objet a*. While the *objet a* is insubstantial and eludes our grasp, eludes even our ability to countenance it, it is also Real, the most real, for Lacan, because it is the anchoring point of our subjectivity. We desire as subjects because the *objet a*, impossible object of desire, the scrap of the Real, causes us to want it. It is both a hole in signification and an attractor. Consequently, it is the site of all striving and all fantasy in the subject's world despite being absent. The Real—the hole in signification—is Lacan's subversion of the Kantian thing. Unlike Derrida, however, Lacan does not bemoan the lost thing and the contradictions it incurs. While Lacan is quick to point out that any attempt to obtain the *objet a* is a fantasy and destined to fail, he, in contrast to Derrida, insists that we do in fact obtain one *thing*, the essential thing: jouissance, or the enjoyment of failure. Thus, there is nothing to lament about failure, and one need not posture as a melancholy deconstructionist, because failure enables us to desire and, what is more, to act on the basis of that desire, regardless of the outcome.

Consequently, *destitution (objet a)* and *institution (desire)* should be read simultaneously as contradictory acts of destruction and return. Although destitution makes the objects of desire impossible, there would be no future and no politics worth fighting for without that impossibility. Loss *gives* substance (albeit a fantasied substance) to an otherwise insubstantial void.

The Return of the Subject

The subject of philosophy has long been considered a dead end—disastrous, by many accounts, totalitarian, according to Max Horkheimer and Theodor Adorno.[33] The death of the subject continues apace in ecological criticism, which champions a desubjectivized, "flat ontology,"[34] contending that the subject represents an idealist, masculinist, white, heteronormative, and anthropocentric point of view. While the subject lives on in these theories, its status is significantly different. The subject is now a transit point for nonhuman materials and toxins, and no longer what it was for Descartes, Jean-Paul Sartre, Lacan, and Badiou: a subjectivized nothing haunting the material world.

While there is no denying that anthropocentrism is a problem and that the dialectic of enlightenment denounced by Adorno and Horkheimer has had devastating consequences for human and nonhuman life, it is questionable whether the subject, defined as a split subject, can be so easily dispatched and whether its removal is indeed beneficial. Heidegger rids the subject of philosophy in favor of Dasein. Adorno excoriates the subject and the whole Enlightenment tradition as a blight on human existence. Graham Harman's object-oriented ontology (or OOO) tries to correct Heidegger's concepts by purging them of their lasting humanism. And various posthuman ecologies put the Cartesian subject on the rack in the name of more-than-human life.

Much of theory today devises ways to escape the so-called prison house of subjectivity, which it considers anthropocentric, reductive, alienated, and torn from the upsurge of existence. Yet theory misses the fact that this very escape or desubjectivizing turn is only possible *because* the subject is a self-eliminating thing. For Hegel, a philosophy of substance (or materialist philosophy broadly) misses the contradiction at play in the subject's relation to itself and the world. In contrast to a philosopher like Heidegger, for whom the being of Dasein is always already being-in-the-world, or an object-oriented philosopher like Graham Harman, who follows Heidegger in subtracting subjectivity from the world of objects, Hegel is less concerned with the supposed despotism of the subject relative to other beings (or Being). That is because, in Hegel's dialectic, the subject is always split. The subject does not impose itself on the world of objects, as Heidegger, Harman, and countless others think. The subject is, according to Hegel, proof that the object, rather than being substantial or undivided, is also split.[35]

When Hegel writes, "Everything turns on grasping and expressing the True, not only as *Substance*, but equally as *Subject*," his point is that substance is not really substantial.[36] Substance is radically broken. That is Hegel's basic point when he declares that substance is equally subject. The point is not, contra Heidegger and OOO, that substance is reducible to subjectivity; the point is that substance and subject share a common divide. Without subjectivity, and here Sartrean existentialism is aligned with Hegel, the world would close in on itself.

The turn to nonhuman worlds beyond the subject avoids this crucial Hegelian lesson. We do not gain access to a world of objects by eliminating subjectivity. We gain access to a world of objects when and only when we realize that the object is equally subject—that is, divided. Otherwise, we would not have access to it.

The undivided noumenon (thing-in-itself) is Kant's legacy. But it is not Hegel's. For Hegel, only a subject divided from its world could begin to imagine a world devoid of subjects. Therein lies the contradiction of Hegel's philosophy—you need a subject to rid the subject. The antinomy of Hegel's thought frees subjectivity to be more than mere substance and delivers thought to the world. Though the current subjectless philosophies view the subject as a problem—a roadblock to vital, emergent, evolutionary, nonwestern, anti-Enlightenment, queer, nocturnal, wild, and subversive substance—Hegel argues just the opposite. Subjectivity reveals the truth of substance, because substance is also subject. The nonhuman world is never more alive, Hegel argues, than when it engenders its own destruction. That contradiction is possible and thinkable because the subject is quintessentially a suicidal animal; by saying "I," I sow my own death.

Blood, Guts, and Automobiles

Despite its reception as a body-horror classic (in the vein of David Cronenberg's films), the horror and splendor of Julia Ducournau's film *Titane* (2021) derive not from its interest in bodily substance but from its insistence, à la Hegel's *Phenomenology*, that substance is equally subject.[37]

We do not grasp a truer or more authentic image of the body by turning to viscera, blood, or bone, as in the body-horror genre, or objects cleaved from subjects, as in OOO. Heidegger's famous phenomenological reading of Van Gogh's boots—the boots that house the Nothing—comes closer to Hegel's split ontology.[38] Yet, for Heidegger, the point of Dasein is to remove the obfuscations of theory—or the stain of subjective mediation—from the object's true being. Despite the many differences among the body-horror genre, object-oriented ontology, and Heidegger's phenomenological reduction, they all have this in common: the removal (or in the case of horror, dismemberment) of the subject.

Heidegger, post-Heideggerians like Harman, and many vitalist thinkers not indebted to Heidegger or OOO share a common interest in the immediacy of substance and view mediation, or the alienation of the signifier, as the greatest threat to ecological belonging. While it is true that signification bars ecological belonging in any straightforward sense, immediacy is the real deception, according to Hegel, since immediacy masks the division of the object. As Hegel shows, even the sense-certainty of the object, for instance, the object "cat," depends on the mediation of the signifiers "cat," "tabby," and "gray" to give the illusion of immediacy. If the cat were not cleaved by mediation, there would be no way and no reason to speak of it. The cat is only interesting because it is not identical—that is, because it is a "cat" and not simply a cat.

Titane is not about cats, sadly. It's about the relationship between sex and death, human and machine, flesh and metal, organic and inorganic, and, in the film's second half especially, masculine and feminine genders. It's about fucking. Specifically, it's about fucking automobiles, which the protagonist—Alexia, later named Adrien (Agathe Rousselle)—does repeatedly, eventually becoming pregnant and giving birth to a human-car hybrid.

The film divides neatly into two parts. The first half deals with Alexia's adolescent trauma resulting from a car accident that leaves her with a titanium plate affixed to her skull and shows her later in life not only attracted to inorganic substances (cars and metal especially) but also willing to murder to satisfy her mechanophilic lust. The more she desires mechanical substance, the higher the body count. In one scene, she dances erotically on and around a show car and seems to derive a high degree of enjoyment from what is ostensibly an exhausting and objectifying job; she gets paid to dance in a bathing suit for the mostly male spectators gathered at the car show. In the very next scene, she stabs one of those male spectators in the neck with a hairpin, killing him in the parking lot before returning indoors, where she is seduced by a gyrating, engine-revving vehicle. She fucks the car passionately, receiving its hydraulic thrusts with bruising satisfaction and with hands and arms restrained by the back seat safety belts. Ducournau films their sex with unapologetic seriousness.

Beyond the superficial comparison to the body-horror genre mentioned above, one thing must be said about the first half of the film that directly contradicts its too-easy association with bodily substance: the film *fails* to resolve the contradiction between flesh and machine. Although Alexia is drawn to mechanical substance, this only leads to her unsustainable murder spree, as if the film's final verdict on the desubjectivized space of object-oriented ontology, in which we are all objects colliding in space, is critique—the less there is of the subject, the more substance becomes overwhelmingly violent.[39]

The second half of the film does not try to reconcile subject and substance (or the relationship between drive and object) but instead reconciles itself to contradiction. The antinomy between human and machine in the first half sustains Alexia's, now Adrien's, self-discovery as subject—that is, a subject riven by difference. It is only when Adrien accepts their alienation from substance that they become open to a world of relations that are human, nonhuman, trans, and anti-Oedipal. (They gain a father, but not their father. The father is, per Lacan, fraudulent.) It's not that the film overcomes body horror in the second half; neither Hegel nor *Titane* believe such a synthesis is possible. Instead, the film shows that substance is necessarily subject, and only a subject divided (not, per Heidegger and Harman, substance divided from subjects) makes room for otherness in the world.

Extimacy

The crucial idea of ecotheory is that we are all connected. I accept this "all" and take it one step further. We are all connected by the lack we share. In this, I cleave the "all" of ecocriticism from itself, making it "not-all" in Lacan's psychoanalytic idiom.[40]

The "not-all" is arguably Lacan's most enigmatic term. For now, I focus on its logic.

Imagine a set including every possible set of species. We will call this mathematical set "Nature." This set would be a fair representative of the all-encompassing immanentism of ecotheory, in which everything is included. Now, imagine a set that does not include itself. See the problem? For a mathematical set to be whole, and all inclusive, one term must stand outside the set. If, for example, you are indexing all the books in a library, the "library's books" would constitute the set, whereas the index would stand awkwardly outside of it. Wouldn't the index, or the book representing all available books, be included in the "all"? How can a book be inside the set of all possible books and yet outside it at the same time?

You have entered Bertrand Russell's paradox. The great mathematician discovered—to the dismay of his contemporaries, who wanted a tidy, whole set—that no set can include itself. The very notion of an inside or complete set falls into contradiction. To be a whole set, an inside, the set must exclude one term (the index in our example above) *while forgetting* that the excluded term must also be included by its own logic.

Lacan takes this logical paradox and runs with it. For Lacan, the goal is not to resolve the paradox, which would be impossible. Thought, he wagers, should take seriously the paradox as the very condition of sense.

"Not-all" is Lacan's signpost for this paradoxical condition in which sense founders. It founders because it is so nonsensical, keeping in mind here the root meaning of *sens*—that is, direction. The library example gives us a clear sense of direction (there are the books inside the library and one book standing nebulously outside it), whereas the "not-all" jumbles in and out. Let's return to our hypothetical. We will call "Nature" the set of all possible existents and "Book of Nature" the index that constitutes the whole from without. From the perspective of the "not-all," this set runs into problems. Not the blissful problems recounted by Duke Senior in *As You Like It*: "Books in the running brooks, / Sermons in stones, and good in everything."[41] The logical paradox would be something more like *Alice in Wonderland*, where books in brooks run in all directions like portmanteaus without a clear sense of direction. Or consider the dream paradox in David Lynch's *Twin Peaks: The Return*. At one point, FBI Deputy Director Gordon Cole (David Lynch) recalls a dream in which Monica Bellucci tells him, "We are like the dreamer who dreams and lives inside the dream, but who is the dreamer?"[42] Lynch's dreamer lives in and outside the dream. This is the paradox of the "not-all."

Political readings of Lacan's *Seminar XX* assert the potential of the "not-all" to explode oppositions between inside and outside, friend and foe, neighbor and monster, and symbiont and virus. Feminists, in particular, have radicalized the "not-all" as a feminine universal in which contradictions run rampant, eroding the masculine ideal of a discrete, bounded identity.[43] Might ecocriticism join the mix?

What I propose is the extimacy of in and out.

Outside: We are menaced by an incognizable wound to ecological thought.

Inside: We are impelled to inflict this wound again and again, because it alone forces thought to think beyond its immanent sphere.

Outside in: We are, according to Lacan's paradoxical logic, never fully inside the set of all natural existents. But neither are we fully outside it. Instead, we in-exist our ecological entanglements. The set of all beings includes an outside, a hole that can never be made a member. The Real-ism of psychoanalysis banks everything on the existence of that hole and the paradox of being both out and in.

2
The Earth Is Evil

Lars von Trier's film *Melancholia* (2011)—though it has become a darling of ecocriticism (more on that momentarily)—serves as a helpful example of the nonrelation as it pertains to ecocriticism.[1] The film begins with an eight-minute-long prologue in which Earth and a previously unknown planet, "Melancholia," move across the screen in what appears like a cosmic opera. During this sequence, Wagner's prelude to *Tristan and Isolde* (1859) plays on the soundtrack. According to Wagner, *Tristan and Isolde* is an opera "of endless yearning, longing, the bliss and wretchedness of love," and this is precisely the tone that von Trier's cosmic opera creates.[2] Manohla Dargis describes the images in von Trier's opening sequence as having "a similar liminal quality in that each refers to an extracted narrative moment, and in-between feelings, sensations, gestures."[3] In one such moment, an image of the film's protagonist, Justine (Kirsten Dunst), appears on the screen, interspersed with outer-space footage. The image is an allusion to John Everett Millais's painting *Ophelia* (1852; figure 1). In the film, Justine lies motionless, floating face up in the water, wearing a wedding dress and clutching a bouquet (figure 2). The wedding dress and bouquet are remnants—shown in prolepsis—of the film's first narrative chapter, in which Justine leaves her newly wedded husband,

FIG. 1. John Everett Millais, *Ophelia* (1852). Source: WikiCommons.

FIG. 2. Still from *Melancholia* (2011).

Michael (Alexander Skarsgård), and flees the constraints of marriage. The image also alludes to Shakespeare's *Hamlet*, specifically the play's tragic heroine, Ophelia.

As the eight-minute-long prologue reaches its climax, the previously unknown planet smashes into Earth. Yet the violence of Earth's destruction is oddly deflationary. When the catastrophe finally happens and everything is destroyed, we are left with the unresolved drama of the two female protagonists, Justine and Claire (Charlotte Gainsbourg). There is no attempt on the part of the characters to prevent the catastrophe, nor is there any possibility of humanity surviving in a postapocalyptic future. If the catastrophe proves important to the narrative at all, it is only to suggest that the real catastrophe has already happened. Bookended by the discovery of the unknown planet on the one hand and its eventual collision with Earth on the other, Justine and Claire's drama dwells in the unresolved—never to be resolved—space of affect and suspense. From a certain perspective, the end of the world has already happened.[4]

In terms of genre, *Melancholia* can best be described as a melodrama.[5] It is a melodrama of extinction. To describe von Trier's film as a melodrama is to move away from any pejorative characterization of the genre and to realize instead that, on the most basic level, melodrama is, as Jonathan Goldberg argues, about the relation of its characters to a "Truth" too intolerable to bear.[6] And because this truth exists in excess of the world, it can only appear as a crack in the world as such. The definitive melodramatic act is, according to Goldberg, that which destitutes the world so that that crack can be widened and truth, however intolerable, can be borne as a result.

Put differently, melodrama is not only or even primarily in the service of world-making. Melodrama, as von Trier imagines it, is a "truth-process" in Alain Badiou's sense—it suspends the world by invoking a truth that this world fatally denies.[7] Badiou calls "evil" the pasting over of a truth (the truth of extinction, for example) with the illusion, enforced on us at any cost, that "we have, if not the good, at least the best possible state of affairs."[8] Here is Badiou speaking on this Leibnizian evil: "Today we see liberal capitalism and its political system, parliamentarism, as the only natural and acceptable solutions. We are made to believe that the global spread of capitalism and what gets called 'democracy' is the dream of all humanity. . . . In truth, our leaders and propagandists know very well that liberal capitalism is an inegalitarian regime, unjust, and unacceptable for the vast majority of humanity."[9] One could criticize Badiou for what appears like a relativist argument: Are there not many culturally specific, context-dependent truths? Doing so would be to miss the point entirely. For Badiou, the point is not that we choose our own truth. Truths (in the plural) are, according to Badiou, universal; they choose us. Love is not true if it does not exceed my demands. Politics is not truly political if it does not exceed the demands of the 1 percent. Evil, therefore, is not an innate condition of the human animal. Instead, "evil is always that which, in a particular situation, tends to weaken or destroy a subject" by suturing that subject to the image of the good—that is, to the belief that this is the best of all possible worlds. Thus, when it comes to the Other and the good that is supposed to come from loving one's others, Badiou is quite clear: "'Respect for the Other' has nothing to do with any serious definition of good and evil."[10] Indeed, being a subject in Badiou's sense means that "very often, it is the 'respect for Others' that is injurious, that is evil."[11]

This is the point at which the question of evil joins necessarily with the question of melodrama. The planet Melancholia in von Trier's film is the quintessential Other. Claire's husband, John (Kiefer Sutherland), cites the scientific community (or rather, *his* scientific community)[12] to offer the most neutral account: The numbers are in, and the determination is that this Other, the previously unknown planet, is good. Melancholia will leave Earth unaffected. "No collision," he repeats. Moreover, the brush with the unknown planet enlivens the would-be scientist, whose position is anything but neutral (Claire says he's "filthy rich," and in truth, he never lets us forget it), filling him with reverence for the dignity of life on Earth. Melancholia reminds John of the fragility of things; life could have been otherwise. When Melancholia changes course in defiance of the scientific projections, John takes his own life. The Other

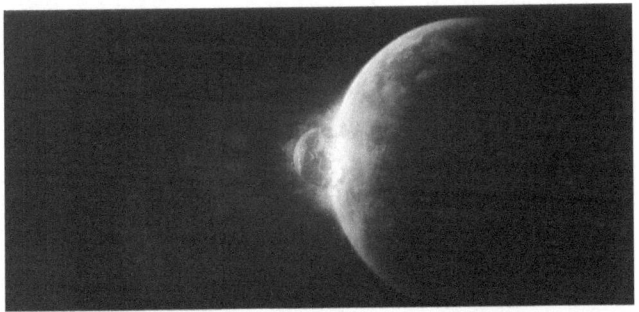

FIG. 3. Still from *Melancholia* (2011).

that had previously filled John with starry-eyed wonder because it confirmed his sense of the world's coherence has become the terrifying Thing, whose closeness ensures Earth's obliteration.

This terror of the Other, good only insofar as it reflects our desired image, is akin to the terror of the (m)Other in psychoanalysis. Freud says that the mother's body (*das Ding*) is the source of all enjoyment and all suffering—all loss.[13] In the film's opening sequence, the collision between Earth and Melancholia forms a single, catastrophic body: two spheres that resemble the maternal breast (figure 3). Here, however, the mother's body becomes an image of total destruction, returning Earth to its original home in mineral death. The relation to this body (planetary and corporeal) is, therefore, not neutral at all, despite John and Claire's attempts to render it so. At one point, Claire says that it looks "friendly."

Recent scholarship on *Melancholia* has echoed Claire's assessment. Bonnie Honig sees in von Trier's film an allegory of the Winnicottian "good enough mother," who provides a "holding environment" capable of withstanding the child's destructive maturation;[14] Claire's child, Leo, serves as an emblem of humanity's struggle with its own fantasied and catastrophic omnipotence.[15] William Connolly, meanwhile, finds in the film a redemptive reminder of the more-than-human world that surrounds us. The film calls to mind the universal "hum" of life.[16]

Justine, by contrast, is an enemy of this "respect for the Other," including the "good enough mother" and the so-called "hum" of our earthly attachments. In response to her sister's plan for a preapocalypse family picnic, Justine says, "You want to meet on the terrace, and sip wine, the three of us?"

CLAIRE: It would make me happy.
JUSTINE: Do you know what I think of your plan?
CLAIRE: No. I was hoping that you might like it.
JUSTINE: I think it's a piece of shit.

Melancholia's collision with Earth determines that all life on Earth is "evil," according to Justine, because it suspends—the film inhabits this suspense—the illusion of the world's coherence. If Melancholia proves to be an obliterating force, evil (to some), because it annihilates the "good" of this world, then Justine takes up cause with this evil by engaging in a truth-process against Mother Earth: "The earth is evil," Justine argues, "we don't need to grieve for it."

Justine's statement flies in the face of environmentalism's Oedipal messaging, which tells us repeatedly that the earth, our "mother," is disappointed in us, that Gaia is upset, and that we better learn to respect our elders and fast. Justine's statement that "the earth is evil" cuts through the false coherence of Mother Earth and finds in it the same absence of full speech that Justine detects in her sister's plan for a family picnic. We tend to think that nature has a plan, that its intentions are good, and that we need only to get back to nature (the "good enough mother") and all will be redeemed. Justine thinks nature's plan is a piece of shit. Why?

For the simple reason that this pretense of coherence masks an underlying incoherence. If *Melancholia* proves important to environmental politics at all, it is because it forces us to think of nature, ourselves, and our tropes of entanglement not as *one side* of a split (good object versus bad object) but as the very *form* of this split. Let us accept the ecological hypothesis that nature is the unconscious condition—metabolism, lifeworld, home—of our blinkered Cartesian existence. Let us also suppose that nature speaks increasingly through disruptions, parapraxes, and uncanny emergencies of world-ending proportion. Nature, in this model, acts as a container or background totality, a defuse mycelium of interacting agencies summoning us to fuller ecological awareness. The problem with this ecological unconscious is that it has nothing at all to do with Freud's theory. The unconscious is, instead, according to Lacan, "impediment, failure, split."[17] It has no other, earthier reality. Nature, if we are to continue the Freudian comparison, isn't a reassuring substance, mother, or container—this was Hegel's insight, discussed in the previous chapter. Nature is not-all, meaning it shares the radical indeterminacy that Freud identifies with the unconscious and that Descartes, the bogeyman of ecotheory, identifies with the *I think*.[18] Contrary to what Timothy Morton says in *Ecology without Nature*, the not-all isn't simply the product of our social construction. If anything, the "unconstructability" of the earth looms large in the chapters of this book.[19] The not-all does not simply mean that there is no nature (after all, fantasies are hard to dispel, even when the object of fantasy is being driven to extinction); not-all means that there is no other world to redeem us.

To say that nature is not-all is to deprive ourselves of a fantasied coherence, which is precisely the fantasy image of the autological subject projected outward, to be reflected back later on.[20] Psychoanalysis teaches us that narcissism works in the future perfect tense: *I will have been that*. My claim is that ecocriticism repeats this basic temporal structure again and again. It splits off all that is bad in the world from an image that it projects into the future, hoping that it will become what, apparently, it already was: *I will have been* an entangled, harmonious nature-culture, a queer mesh, or a saturated, blue vast. But the funny thing about the Lacanian mirror stage is that it isn't a "stage" at all; it is the perpetual motion of life. And it is exhausting. The earth, our big Other, is illusory.

It is time we divest from environmentalism's big Other and put into praxis an environmentalism without image.[21] It is time we learn, after Justine, to destitute the earth.

Against Ecological Holism

Justine's destituent statement, "the earth is evil," isn't a reformist claim. It does not speak to our better natures. The earth is "evil" with respect to a truth-process that determines life on Earth, driven by parasitic capitalism, anti-Blackness, and reproductive humanism, is evil. The affect that dominates *Melancholia* is fatigue. The question for Justine is not: How do I reconcile with the world? For Justine, the problem is quite different. Justine has had *too much* of the world; she's exhausted by it. What is more, she views the world as a global suicide. "There is only life on Earth," Justine intones, "and not for long." The truth of extinction, guaranteed by Earth's collision with Melancholia, melodramatizes a death that has already happened in Justine's view. Formally speaking, Melancholia is a reminder of the inorganic life from which all life on Earth originally sprung and to which all life returns in Freud's speculative theory of the death drive. As if to melodramatize the Anthropocene condition that "geologic man" now faces, *Melancholia* positions the viewer between two deaths, between the prehistoric life of inorganic materialism and the inorganic life that now chokes our biosphere in the form of runaway carbon emissions. Trauma happens in twos, Freud argues. Von Trier's melodrama constitutes what we might call the long "detour" (though it has accelerated dramatically in the last few decades) that life takes to return to the inorganic.

In terms of affect, then, fatigue is the objective affect of life on Earth. Being exhausted by the world isn't, according to *Melancholia*, a private emotion but rather a general structure of feeling affecting all life. In calling this world, the world of 24/7 accumulation, "evil," Justine not only critiques the global structure of fatigue, where all life and all manner of busyness is but a detour toward inorganic death, but also destitutes that structure, rendering the global structure of fatigue inoperative.

What manner of life breaks from life itself? According to Freud, drive sexuality (*Trieb*) breaks from the vital order (the order of fatigue) by splitting life into two. Neither the perpetuation of biological life (fatigue) nor the return to inorganic matter (mineral death) constitutes the work of the drive. Rather, drive is a form of suspension or delay; it gets off by putting off a final satisfaction. As Alenka Zupančič explains, "Satisfaction (for the sake of satisfaction) is not the goal of the drive, but its *means*. This is what is profoundly disturbing about the 'death drive': not that it wants only to enjoy, even if it kills us, but that it wants only to repeat this negativity, the gap in the order of being, *even if this means to enjoy*."[22] The same could also be said of melodrama—the melodramatic subject qua subject of the drives breaks with the vital order. Drive repeats the "gap" in enjoyment, which is another way of saying that it prolongs life's pleasurable-unpleasurable tensions, including the in-between states that melodrama spectacularizes. This definition of drive bears a striking resemblance to Thomas Elsaesser's definition of melodrama as "a system of punctuation," one that gives "expressive colour and chromatic contrast to the storyline" by creating "certain moods" such as "sorrow, violence, dread, suspense, happiness."[23] As "a system of punctuation," melodrama suspends forward action so that affect can well to the surface. What may look like mere inaction at the level of the plot gives rise to, in Goldberg's words, "states of hesitation, musical irresolution, cross-purpose, key change, suspension, and half-voicing [that] are themselves kinds of knowledge."[24] Suspended between two deaths, drive circles endlessly around a gap in the vital order. It peels away from the vital order by enjoying the little death or the little nothing that life sutures with its endless command to *enjoy!*

Although the first chapter of *Melancholia* is titled "Justine," it could just as well be titled "Enjoy!" because the command to enjoy saturates Justine's whole world, from the world of the wedding party to the world of commerce. Her boss, an advertising executive, tries to squeeze one more "tagline" out of her before the party is over. Here, enjoyment and fatigue blur together. Life, love, and the pursuit of happiness are advertising slogans in the world of the film.

But the truth of extinction ruptures this alliance between enjoyment and fatigue. Mineral death, the film shows us, has already happened to life on Earth. It was always bound to happen. Anyone who pretends otherwise is, in Justine's view, "evil," not because of a surplus of sadism on Justine's part (though her name is a reference to the novel *Justine* by Marquis de Sade), but because the truth of extinction makes life and the command to enjoy it, even if it kills us, exhausting. By contrast, Justine's response isn't the progressive choice, which reactivates the liberal humanist subject by commanding it to enjoy life *better*— that is, less rapaciously (witness the Green New Deal); Justine's response is fully melodramatic, in that it finds freedom, tenderness, and love, in destitution. Neither hedonistic enjoyment nor "new deal" self-maintenance, melodrama, as figured by Justine, wills the self's extinction to put off (infinitize, delay) mineral death. *Justine lives death differently.*

This book calls for a different end of the world and does so not only by echoing the words of Justine in *Melancholia* but also in complicity with those who are mapping worlds outside of and in the fault lines of this one—"in the break," as Fred Moten puts it.²⁵ These complicities are not univocal. Ending white supremacy is not the same as ending worker alienation, for example, a point too often forgotten by Marxist critics. The same goes for ending heteropatriarchy, a system of oppression that exists in tension with these others. The "woman question," that map of the unknown drawn by Freudian psychoanalysis in the late nineteenth and early twentieth centuries, is still a stumbling block insofar as "woman" remains a problem for all subject positions. According to Andrea Long Chu, femaleness isn't a way of being *in* the world; it is that which the world desperately guards *against*. What's more, *we are all female*, Chu argues: "Castration happens *on both sides* [male and female]."²⁶

Similarly, Frank B. Wilderson III shows that Blackness is not analogous with feminist and class-based subject positions—contrary to the rhetoric of intersectionality and multiculturalism. Blackness is not *of* this world; Blackness, according to Wilderson, is what the world refuses to *become*.²⁷

My goal is not to harmonize these arguments. Nor am I trying to posit a universal ground, much less a common humanity. It is the very notion of a "common humanity" that is being called into question here. What I am positing, instead, after Justine, is a universal fracture or discord. What is common to Black, Indigenous, and LGBTQ struggles isn't the ground "we all" stand on but the discord we share. Chu underscores this point in her book *Females*, where she claims that the only true universal, the only "thing" that binds everyone, is lack (castration), which the word "female" in her argument represents.²⁸

By and large, ecocriticism has taken flight from signifiers of lack. Castration, as a concept, doesn't even make it in the front door of the *oikos*. But if lack exists, ecocriticism tells us, it is because of capitalism. Lack is what happens *to* an original fullness of life, ecology, and embodied humanism. Even our ecomelancholia becomes a vehicle for reaffirming an original (read: more authentic) holism. In one influential example of eco-Marxism, Jason W. Moore's *Capitalism in the Web of Life*, we read that "we"—humanity as a whole—are enmeshed with nature. Humanity isn't outside nature, Moore argues; we are rather in "nature as a flow of flows."[29] This, of course, is in opposition to the two-substance ontology of René Descartes, whose mind-body dualism Moore posits as the catalyst of all that's wrong in the world. To begin to undo the capitalist world system, we must, Moore argues, train ourselves to see capital as an *interruption* to the web of life. For, as Moore argues, we *are* this "web." The path to abundance begins with reclaiming the "*oikeios*," our home.[30]

Moore's "web of life" is a rich and persuasive analysis of deleterious capitalism, but it leaves no room for the destituent act.[31] And that is because Blackness, femaleness, queer, trans, and Indigenous subjectivity, these forms of life are not just interrupted *by* capitalism; they *are* the interruption. They interrupt the coherence that capitalism seeks to impose, as well as the "web of life" that white Marxism would put in its place. But life isn't a harmonious web. The violence of worlds isn't the result of a forced disruption to the web of life; if anything, it is a forced coherence that activist groups like Black Lives Matter are protesting when they say, "We can't breathe." The web of life is stifling.

As an alternative to life under capital, Moore, like many Marxist ecologists, posits our world relations, our ties, as the image of a "truer us." In other words, Moore calls on the constituency of the human and more-than-human to assemble and build a better lifeworld. What does this constituency leave out?

What it leaves out, namely, is the destituency itself. For the destituent is always less than *one*. What makes up the destitute? It is the fact that we affirm our lack as a *positive* difference. Instead of the interrelationship of all things, we uphold the lack of relation (similar to Lacan's formula on sex: "There's no such thing as a sexual relation") as relationality's main drive.[32] Instead of unifying under the yoke of the *oikeios* (Moore's version of the Gaia hypothesis), we, the destitute, along with Justine, consider the earth, and all its vocations of life, evil; instead of externalizing lack as an outside force, something that happens *to* an original fullness, we affirm lack as the only ground on which to stand. What makes up the destitute? It is the fact that we are not trying to save the earth.

Against the World

When contemporary disaster films imagine the end of the world, they imagine a singular tragedy. The Western, capitalist, white, heteronormative world ends—yet it is saved by narratives of rebuilding.[33] By contrast, *Melancholia* imagines the end as little more than a domestic chamber drama, where everyday life turns violently on Justine's hatred for this world. Why?

Let us defamiliarize our terms momentarily by turning to Freud's interrogation of the role of the mother, the first Other, in the libidinal constitution of the subject. The mother (we will allow conventional gendering for now) attends to the child's needs from birth and is, for that reason, the first somatic contact with the outside world. Unfortunately, for the child and us, this means that one must learn to communicate and enter a common communicative network. The symbolic is this communicative structure, which the infant learns to occupy, albeit not without difficulty. Two consequences follow. First, the mother, as source of satisfaction, is no longer whole. A common communicative language can never fully capture the mother in her totality. As the child learns to communicate with others in a shared medium, the senseless jouissance of the mother's body, which is incomparable, falls away. The mother's body is split between recognizable signifiers, on the one hand, and the alien Thing (jouissance of the body), on the other, which no signifier can capture. This (non)relation to the mother's body splits the world into two. Not only is the child's sensory apparatus unable to grasp the mother as a whole object, but the mother is also alien to herself. In her actions, sounds, pleasures, and partings, the mother is awash in enigmatic signifiers, which make her alien (unconscious) to the child and herself. The being of the mother is, therefore, originally crossed out: ~~mother~~.

The so-called loss of the Thing is a retrospective illusion or fantasy on the part of the indefatigable child, who necessarily believes that there is somewhere an object that will fill the lack of the maternal Thing. I say *necessarily* because without that belief, there would be nothing and no reason to desire. The alien mother causes the child to desire, and what the child wants is the answer to the mother's riddle, which also becomes the child's: What do I (or this other, this alien within me) want? The temporality and becoming of the child's desire are the temporality of this question mark, this unconscious gap. One of subjectivity's central challenges, then, at least from the perspective of psychoanalysis, is to learn how to act on the basis of this gap, on the baselessness of human desire. If desire is no longer for something or someone, then we are left with the seemingly empty result that it is for nothing. Both Freud and Lacan challenge us to see this nothing askew, for it is not that the object of desire becomes a matter of indifference. On the contrary, the object of desire becomes singularly important to the precise extent that it supports the failure of the Thing—that is to say, insofar as it lets us *enjoy* the Thing. This, according to Lacan, is the true meaning of love: I love my object not because of what it represents or for the satisfaction it promises but because it is immediately satisfying. It is satisfying in that it lets me relive the partial satisfaction of the Thing. The love object incarnates the Thing as a form of destitution so that my relation to the love object becomes, uniquely, a nonrelation: I love in you something more than you, Lacan writes. Although this endorsement of the nonrelation is, on the surface, narcissistic, it is also radically impersonal; for where the partial object or the fragment of maternal nonbeing emerges, "I" am not. The "I" only exists as an illusion of totality, of full being, whereas the partial object as the seat of the partial drive is asubjective and impersonal; it reduces "me" to nothing, to the alien (m)Other that is (in) me more than me. Love is the great impersonalizer.

Claire Denis's film *Stars at Noon* (2022) is, like Lacan's and Badiou's theory, radically oriented by its method of subtraction.[34] The film gives the spectator very little anchorage in the world of its characters. There are two main characters. One is a woman, Trish (Margaret Qualley), who may or may not be a journalist and who sells her body for money. The other is a man, Daniel (Joe Alwyn), who may or may not be a hired gun, who may or may not be a secret agent, and whose life is in danger for unknown reasons. As spectators, we know even less than the main characters, because we have no direct access to their pasts or thoughts. They could be lying, and they probably are. All we know is that they are in love. They profess it. Of course, that could also be a lie, but the severity of the events that unfold in the film and the dangers they incur as lovers suggest their fidelity and the veracity of their love. In Badiou's terms, they are subjects *to* the event of love.

We, too, are in the midst of their love event, as the bulk of the film concerns their attraction to the unnameable (because unknowable) something in the other. They ask almost nothing of each other: who they are, where they are from, what they are doing. They dispense with these questions early on. When the love event seizes them, all else, including the typical diegetic information supplied by narrative film, fades away.

The love event, the film suggests, is radical—radical, in part, because it puts them beyond the grasp of the given situation, which Badiou defines as the "count-as-one" governing capitalist existence. Their identities are enigmatic and remain so because the love event, after it has exerted its force, expels them from the situation. The love event subtracts the lovers from the situation, including the narrative situation of the film. Or rather, it subtracts what they are (subjects of the event) from where they are (their emplotment), delivering them from the space of the place (or "splace," as Badiou calls it) to the "outplace," from which love emerges.[35]

Badiou's post-Freudian intervention in the politics of the Other hinges on this something more. Being a subject of truth means, first, that neither the Other nor the good it represents is ever neutral. The child in Freud's account is already in a truth-process (Badiou); it isn't a neutral relation between mother and child but one in which the child is already subjected to a truth (the mother's desire) in excess of the situation. How to relate to the mother's desire, which may be malignant to the child's freedom, depends entirely on this truth-process, which, we know after Freud, is interminable. Being a subject of truth means, second, that "very often, it is the 'respect for Others' that is injurious, that is evil." On this point, Badiou cites Marguerite Duras: "Duras has recounted how, for reasons tied to the resistance to the Nazis, she participated in acts of torture against traitors. The whole distinction between good and evil arises from inside a becoming-subject, and varies with this becoming (which I myself call philosophy, the becoming of a truth)."[36] Or as we saw in Freud, the whole distinction arises from inside a relation to the (m)Other, where becoming-subject means separating from the Other and affirming that which is universally true: the mother/other/world is not-all. Although the subject takes pleasure in linking and forging new relations between meanings and perceptions and in extending these meanings out into the future, the ground of every relation is a nonrelation—what Badiou calls the rupture of a "truth" event—which disjoins every object and meaning from itself. Like the melancholic in Freud's essay "Mourning and Melancholia," the subject of truth repeats a fundamental dissatisfaction because she enjoys the loss (of self) that repetition sustains. This impossible satisfaction is the true, silent source of my enjoyment. What I enjoy in the object is its division, its relation to an impossible whole. The question for Badiou's subject is thus: How, against all manner of evils, do I relate to this other evil, the something in me that is more than me qua truth, my closest neighbor?[37]

Like Freud's melancholic, the destitution I examine in these pages attests to profound loss. However, closer to Freud's true insight in "Mourning and Melancholia," the destitution I speak of does *not know* what it has lost. Loss is a devilish thing, because it is never self-evident. Freud's point about melancholia was not the everyday platitude that we all suffer from losses; his precise point was that we all suffer from the difficulty of identifying—of putting into words—our loss. Melancholia, precisely put, is the affective correlative of the *loss of loss*. Although I say I have lost x, I don't know what I have lost in x. This additional cloud of unknowing differentiates mourning from melancholia and makes the melancholic protest so discordant, so unresolvable. Freud writes,

> One cannot see clearly what has been lost, and it is all the more reasonable to suppose that the patient cannot consciously perceive what he has lost either. This, indeed, might be so even if the patient is aware of the loss which has given rise to his melancholia, but only in the sense that

he knows *whom* he has lost but not *what* he has lost in him. This would suggest that melancholia is in some way related to an object-loss which is withdrawn from consciousness, in contradistinction to mourning, in which there is nothing about the loss that is unconscious.[38]

I believe this is at the heart of Wilderson's destituent statement: "We're trying to destroy the world."[39] Not a desire to redeem loss by putting something new in its place. And not a desire to destroy for the sake of it. But a desire to *make a place for loss*—losses without a name.[40] Blackness, for Wilderson, isn't something that can be added to the (white) world; it is what names the (white) world's impossibility (its lack of itself).

Death Driven

When Freudo-Marxism in the twentieth century—from Herbert Marcuse to Deleuze and Guattari to Juliet Mitchell—tried marrying a Marxist politics of emancipation to Freudian psychoanalysis, it was the early Freud of the repressed sexual drive that these theorists turned to. The reason is simple. The repressed sexual drive maps nicely onto a theory of emancipation; release the sexual drive, these thinkers posit, and the revolution will follow. Todd McGowan stresses, however, that psychoanalytic politics only truly emerges after Freud discovers the death drive. This discovery has proven much harder to integrate with leftist politics. As McGowan writes, "The death drive has historically acted as a stumbling block for psychoanalytic politics because it involves our self-sabotage. It leads us to work unconsciously against social betterment."[41] He adds that the death drive is "an essentially masochistic structure within the psyche."[42]

My claim is that the environmental Left underestimates the libidinal value of this masochistic structure in building large-scale coalitional politics. Although the Left knows much about sacrificing *for* the good, it has a narrow view of enjoyment. For Freud, the progressive view of enjoyment gets things all wrong. Loss, he argues, isn't incidental to the good; it is necessary. For Freud, loss produces a barrier to satisfaction, and that barrier or limit, that cognitive impasse, is immediately enjoyable.

Although one can never make the death drive conscious, one can imagine a libidinal politics that makes space for the destituting force of the drive. Psychoanalytic criticism has not been especially good at arising to this imaginative challenge. While Lee Edelman's *No Future* sets the bar for death-driven politics, it brands the death drive as inherently apolitical. Indeed, insofar as the death drive is counterintuitive to politics, it is not unmerited that Edelman theorizes queerness as a form of symbolic destitution, a way of exiting from the symbolic order and turning the father's "no" back on the white, cis, hetero, patriarchal order. Death drive, for Edelman, is the "no" of politics insofar as politics writ large is unthinkable beyond the axis of fantasy. And because the death drive, for Freud, names this beyond, a beyond that no political project can master or contain, the death drive must be, per Edelman, the death of politics.

I affirm this Edelmanian "no" as an ineluctable hitch in libidinal economy. However, I add one simple caveat: the "no" of negation is dialectically inconceivable without phantasmatic support—that is, without a positive project to anchor the subject's destitution. I am interested, therefore, like Zupančič, McGowan, and Mari Ruti in imagining a psychoanalytic politics that can lend conceptual support *to* emancipatory struggles while remaining fully faithful to the destituting force of the drive.[43] Put simply, I am interested in the *life* of the death drive. Hence, I have tried throughout this chapter to hang several concepts like ill-fitting garments on the cadaver of libidinal economy. Those concepts include the uncountable, the part that has no part, the nonrelation, and the destituent act. In

The Earth Is Evil 45

Melancholia, the drive's destituting power is constituted through the figure of Justine.

Justine acts *out*, but she does not act *for*. If anything, her protest against the earth is a protest against forward action, and her *inaction* makes her contemptible to others. Justine rejects her husband, forsakes her family, deserts the pathologies of love, refuses to comply with the demands of her employer, scorns happiness, turns our ecological attachments into a spectacle of human passivity before the blind events of nature, acts with ruthless contempt for the wishes of her sister, Claire, mocks the authority of others, and is indifferent, at best, to the destruction of life on Earth. Worse still, she is inconsolably depressed. Justine's attack on the bourgeois world surrounding her affirms discontinuity over the violence of the world's coherence. *Melancholia* formalizes this discontinuity by beginning *after* the end; it is, in effect, between two deaths that the film's action takes place.

Compare this, the zone between two deaths in *Melancholia*, to its cinematic master, Stanley Kubrick's *2001: A Space Odyssey* (1968), and we begin to see what is at stake, philosophically speaking, in the former.[44] It is obvious that *Melancholia* derives its outer space tableau from *2001*. What is less obvious are the philosophical coordinates underpinning both. Recall the humorous opening sequence in which the newlyweds, Justine and Michael, try navigating a winding dirt road to the afterparty at her sister's estate. Because the stretch limousine is too long, the driver cannot make the necessary turn; while Justine and Michael both take turns behind the wheel, the drive remains comically futile, like driving a square peg through a round whole. One might be giving von Trier too much credit by suggesting that the limousine represents the failure of the drive to reach its target, were it not for the fact that this failure, which makes the newlyweds terribly late, repeats. The drive, represented by the worthless automobile, fails to arrive on time. From this failure, however, it hits a static object: enjoyment. Arguably, the whole cosmic melodrama does nothing more than repeat this initial sequence. Is it not a question throughout the film of Melancholia moving around Earth's trajectory? When it becomes clear that, like the limousine, no such circumvention is possible, Justine and others confront a terrible limit.

We confront the limit also. As spectators, we know that the event of obliteration has already happened. The structure of the film is split along two axes: the axis of fantasy, which narrativizes the gaps in the subject's enjoyment (e.g., the limousine will arrive; Melancholia will pass us by; "No collision"), and the axis of iteration, which repeats an inaugural, catastrophic trauma.[45] To be a subject of the drive, then, according to the film, is to be temporally at odds with oneself, death driven, and undermined at every step. Adrian Johnston's temporal autopsy of the drive lends credence to one of Lacan's more vexing formulas (vexing, that is, from the standpoint of progressivism), that "every drive is virtually a death drive."[46] Subjects cling to fantasy, Johnston argues, precisely to avoid the terrifying negativity of the drive, its pulsive iterability, however repressive or stifling the fantasy. Drive, properly conceived, isn't a cauldron of repressed sexuality waiting to be let loose, as Marcuse and others in the Freudo-Marxist tradition thought. Drive is the unsurpassable temporal obstacle in the way of the subject's fulfillment.

2001: A Space Odyssey is again master and forebear in this regard. Does it not begin, comically, with the creation of the first tool (a bone used to bludgeon others) and end, tragically, with the failure of humanity's tools, frighteningly realized in the murderous supercomputer HAL? It is only after astronaut David Bowman (Keir Dullea) destroys HAL (by dislodging the computer's memory disks) that Dave encounters "authentic" temporality (that is, time unmastered by any human tool:

bone, computer, or otherwise) in the film's final hallucinatory sequence, ending with Bowman's simultaneous death and rebirth. There has never been a more Heideggerian film. From the thesis on tool-being to the final encounter with time as being-toward-death, *2001* distills in cinematic form the Heideggerian and post-Heideggerian obsession with time and death as the ultimate horizons of human finitude and the breaking of humanity's tools as life's proper opening onto vitality, performativity, becoming, *différance*.[47] When the supercomputer breaks in *2001* and Dave confronts his being-toward-death in the simultaneity of past, present, and future, then and only then, the film suggests, are we, with Bowman, reborn.

Melancholia transforms this Heideggerian odyssey. What happens when the limousine gets stuck and Earth is on its fatal trajectory despite all the scientific projections? The result isn't a more authentic experience of time. The result is atemporal: Justine sitting around, inactive; Claire, hopelessly wanting to plan a dinner party, à la Mrs. Dalloway, but confronting absolute stasis. The interval between two deaths is to be understood not as inaugurating a new time, a more authentic time, but time as radical disjunction or cut, severing time and continuity completely. At the bottom of everything, *Melancholia* wagers, is not authentic time—that is, being-toward-death or the differencing profusion of life—but rather impasse, blunder, and stasis. The true existential question, for Freud, isn't: What is to be done with my being-toward-death? Rather it's: What is to be done with my terrible enjoyment, which is too much for me, which does not budge? The Freudian rejoinder to Heideggerian and post-Heideggerian ex-stasis is this: You have not dealt with the atemporality of desire; you have not yet dealt with the extimacy of the unconscious. As Lacan reminds us, the unconscious knows no season, no past, and no death. It is, instead, a cut, the enjoyment of which carves up time, making

FIG. 4. Still from *Melancholia* (2011).

FIG. 5. Still from *Melancholia* (2011).

life discontinuous. Thus, whereas *2001* gives us Heideggerian tragedy (our tools become the very instruments of our downfall and rebirth), *Melancholia* gives us Chaplinesque enjoyment. Destitute of everything, including time, Justine and company become cosmic Tramps. Their challenge, and ours, is to enjoy the limit, or the hitch (difficulty, snag, interruption, barrier), of the drive.

And enjoy it they do. Moments before the previously unknown planet Melancholia crashes into Earth, we see one of the most beautiful if fragile representations of leftist solidarity rendered in film—Justine; her sister, Claire; and Claire's son, Leo, who nicknames Justine "Auntie Steel Breaker," sit in a triangular formation shielded by little more than a stick-figure enclosure (figures 4 and 5). Justine calls it the "magic cave."

After so many attempts to resignify Earth's obliteration through appeals to science, knowledge, family, art, and love—after so many attempts to quilt the catastrophe of Melancholia—Claire and Leo shelter in the magic cave that Justine has been destituting (that is, setting up [de + *statuĕre*]) throughout the film. The structure is *magic*, because it works to bring Justine, Claire, and Leo together in concert around the lack they share. It is a *cave* because the magic that binds Justine and company *is* the magic of this lack, the hollow left when all else has been evacuated. The power of the film's final scene derives from the fact that Justine stands inside the hollow. What is more, she invites others to join her inside the magic cave, although it is an "inside" that makes no distinction between in and out (the cave is radically open).

Framed inside the magic cave, Justine adopts a nickname: Auntie Steel Breaker. The nickname means nothing, given that no amount of strength, familial bond, or steely eyed courage will stop Earth's destruction. There are no breaks. And yet this failure to mean anything is exactly what makes the nickname relevant, politically speaking, to Zupančič. In defining the nickname, Zupančič asks,

> An example of a signifier that would prevent the gap of the "impossible" from simply disappearing from the scene (and returning in the Real)? Could we not say that a possible example of this would be the way in which a nickname sometimes functions in love relationships? And by this I do not mean a "cute name" that one can pick from a list of such names, I mean a name that really names something in the relationship; a name that provides the signifier of the very (dis)junction of love object and existing object in a concrete love relationship.

FIG. 6. Still from *Melancholia* (2011).

> A name that works, works at generating and maintaining the *space* for construction at the precarious *point* of the Event. Such (nick)names . . . usually have a comic sparkle to them, and this sparkle goes some distance in distracting the pathos of love as *destiny*.[48]

The nickname, like the master signifier (aka phallus or Name-of-the-Father), is impotent. Crucially, though, the nickname reveals its impotency; it makes its castration *known*.

When Auntie Steel Breaker invites Claire and Leo inside the magic cave, she divulges the impotency of the nickname. The cave is a flimsy structure, structured by and giving structure to the void. But it is a *structure* nonetheless. Justine invites others to shelter in it and make the void the basis of left solidarity (figure 6).

What's left for Justine, Claire, and Leo in the end? Not much. Theirs is an impossible future. The beauty and brutality of *Melancholia* are announced in the opening sequence, in a collision that makes the remainder of the film null. We, for the remainder of the film, are left to inhabit that void, even if, narratively speaking, we retreat from it. Refusing to retreat, refusing to cede desire for the lost object any longer, Justine builds a structure out of nothing and gathers solidarity around the minus, the lack they share, as if to say, *Comrades in lack, let's do the impossible.*

Although it has been said that *Melancholia* is a film about endings,[49] the opposite is true: never in the history of cinema has the end been so radically conceived as a beginning—that is to say, the impossible happened . . . now what?

3

Zero-Waste Sex and Other Energy Fictions

On Earth Day, April 22, 2021, environmental activist Greta Thunberg released a video on social media with the hashtag #MindTheGap. The #MindTheGap hashtag quickly entered the mainstream of environmental discourse as a reminder of the ever-widening gap between real decarbonization efforts and the current state of fossil fuel dependency throughout the world. Thunberg's #MindTheGap video begins like so many viral videos on the internet. It begins with kittens. Only, this video isn't just catnip for nature lovers. No sooner are we met with fuzzy kittens than an error message appears on-screen: "Warning! Signal Lost."[1] Cut to Thunberg standing in a field of clear-cut timber. A mixture of glitch cinematography, hypermontage, and meme aesthetics, the #MindTheGap video dispenses with feel-good nature imagery and confronts the reader with visual agitation. Each fragmentary image casts the pastoral kitten back into the realm of the imaginary before collapsing back into its own interstitial chaos. The video is hypermediated and hyperconsumerist and points to the current state of climate breakdown, which is happening at a frenetic pace compared to current decarbonization efforts. At the center of the visual frame, Thunberg narrates the dilemma: "On Earth Day 2021, at the Leaders' Climate Summit, countries will present their new climate commitments. Like 'net zero emissions by 2050.' They will call these hypothetical targets 'ambitious.' But, when you compare our insufficient targets with the overall current best available science, you clearly see that there's a gap. There are decades missing."[2] The swiftest plans for decarbonization are still not fast enough. The worst carbon offenders, including the United States, propose net-zero greenhouse gas emissions by 2050, a figure that relies heavily on nonexistent carbon-capturing technology. It is a fool's bargain, Thunberg argues. Moreover, it leaves billions of people exposed to the worst climate outcomes. Thunberg adds, "These targets could be a great start, if it wasn't for the fact that they are full of gaps and loopholes.... The gap between what we are doing and what needs to be done is widening by the minute. And the gap between the urgency needed and the current level of awareness and attention is becoming more and more absurd."[3] Days after the #MindTheGap video was released, President Joe Biden outlined his vision for a decarbonized future. In stark contrast with the Trump administration, which had rejected the 2015 Paris Climate Agreement of 1.5°C global warming and framed the Green New Deal as a threat to the U.S. economy and workers, Biden pledged to cut U.S. greenhouse gas emissions by at least half by 2030. According to Biden, decarbonization is not only "a moral imperative, an economic imperative," but also a temporal one. "We are at an inflection point in history," Biden states.[4] The time to act is now. "If we act to save the planet, we can create millions of jobs and economic growth and opportunity." We can turn "peril into possibility. Crisis into opportunity."[5]

Contrary to Biden's green capitalist agenda, Thunberg urges viewers to *stay in the crisis*—to mind the gap. "This gap of awareness, action and time"—awareness, action, and time being the obvious targets of the #MindTheGap video's fragmentary aesthetic—"is the biggest elephant that has ever found itself in any room," Thunberg deadpans.[6] As the video's four minutes and twenty-three seconds count down, counting itself becomes central to the video's environmental message. The #MindTheGap video holds leaders accountable for the time they have wasted and continue to waste by burning fossil fuels.

Still, between Biden's gapless politics and Thunberg's emphasis on the ever-widening gap of "awareness, action and time," there is a short circuit: Biden's green capitalist subject and Thunberg's enlightened subject are both gapless subjects promising to suture time, action, and awareness together; both try closing the gap between scientific facts and petrofictions.[7]

Of course, Biden's answer is market driven; it relies on the invisible hand of the market to shift toward renewable-energy technology. Biden, a green capitalist, relies on currently existing fossil infrastructure to abracadabra its way to a clean technological future. Meanwhile, Thunberg, who cites all the correct scientific data, says nothing about capitalism directly. While these voices differ substantially, they agree on one thing: there's no time to waste. Ecorealism, in these cases, is a matter of reality *testing*—testing the gap between reality and fiction, margin and error. Reality testing for the ecorealist is the same as it was for Freud, a way of reconciling ourselves to the gaps in our field of vision, to the fact that the hyperobjects of the Capitalocene are never just this cloud, this plastic Coke bottle, or this pipeline, but all the above and more simultaneously.[8] Ecorealism minds the gap by bringing a hyper, glitched, hopelessly fragmentary Earth into view, one image at a time.

And yet there is a critical difference between this version of reality testing and Freud's. In Freud's theory of reality testing, reality is filled not just with hyperobjects but, more frightening still, hypo-objects or nothing-objects, objects that have no interior, that gape open—not simply because they are too vast or too interconnected but because the nothing of hypo-objects incurves the world of thought around it. In Jacques Lacan's radicalization of Freud, the Real is not beside or outside the fiction of ideology but rather inside it, Mobius-like, in the pockets, crevices, interstices, and holes that reality, as a complement to the fictions of ideology, pastes over. Gaze, in Lacan's work, is the objectified form of this nothing-object (scrap or remainder) within the field of vision.[9] This dislocation of the gaze entails a radical disorientation of realist politics. For it is no longer conceivable, after Freud, that thought can pull back the veil of ideology to witness the real. This version of thought is, as Jennifer Friedlander argues, ideology at its finest: "We must go beyond the view of deception as a lie that is presented in the form of truth—a dissimulation in which something pretends to be something it is not. This position limits us to making comparisons between one entity and another in order to assess their similarities and differences. Instead, the deception that will interest us . . . is one which helps us to appreciate internal contradictions—ruses that provoke us to consider the relation a thing has, not with another thing, but rather with itself."[10] In Friedlander's Lacanian film theory, realism colludes with the imaginary. To conceive otherwise would be to fall prey to metalanguage—to the idea that there exists, behind the imaginary, a real outside discursivity. This belief in metalanguage puts ecorealism in a difficult position. For the new materialist or ecorealist, "vibrant matters" zip across the visual spectrum, impressing us with their lively agency.[11] This anarchic materialism is supposed to bring about the reality that an imperious false consciousness keeps at bay. On the contrary, it is this compact between lively matters and the idea of the real as an unmediated upsurge that holds tight to the imaginary, to false consciousness, because it takes the real to be that which we see, not what we fail to see or unsee. In this way, ecorealism gives ground to capitalist futurity; it makes it so that it is easier to imagine the end of the world than the end of our self-certainty.

Both Biden and Thunberg echo Karl Marx's famous critique of philosophy: for too long, philosophers have only thought about the world; the point is to change it.[12] I want to turn this argument around. For too long, the environmental Left has only tried to change the world; the point is to think it. If, as Marx suggests, there is something inherently wasteful about thought, I want to push this observation to its limit. In what follows, I tarry with the notion that thought, particularly cinematic thought about the real, is a corrective to waste. My counterargument is this: thought wastes itself.[13] It is both thanatological and ecological at once. This negativity of thought is what is intolerable to both ecologism and fossil capitalism alike. By mapping the relations among waste, libidinal energy, and aesthetics, this chapter not only brings sex to the surface of energy critique, where it has long been submerged, but also frames thought (particularly cinematic thought) as an explosive energy conduit with shattering consequences.

Mind the Gap

Changing how we think about waste is a far bigger challenge than the energy humanities and environmental humanities typically suppose. From the point of view of the environmental Left, capitalism's endless extraction of surplus value and the immiseration of the worker is fixable. "We can have nice things," concludes Kate Aronoff in *Overheated*.[14] Aronoff's point is hard to dispute. We can, indeed, work less, shop less, and still enjoy things like leisure time, community, and sex. Aronoff's reference is to the sexual *act*; there can be more of it, *if* we uncouple sex from the work-waste dyad, which places value on work alone, and insist on the value of profitless expenditure. Aronoff, like so many leftist environmentalists, pulls back the veil of capitalist ideology to show that human happiness does not depend on having an endless variety of petroproducts. If we were really acting in the planet's (and our own) best interest, we would divest from fossil capitalism immediately. We'd be having *good* sex, lots of it.

Taking up a similar line of thought is Cara New Daggett in *The Birth of Energy*. Echoing Thunberg, Daggett writes, "The gap is widening between the slow pace of human change and the self-amplifying and irreversible geological and planetary feedback loops."[15] Contributing to this gap is the ecomodernist commitment to combating waste through counting, measuring, and energy saving. As Daggett explains, this post hoc way of "proving" that waste and pollution are harmful "requires that humans know about the waste in the first place, and that they can develop the tools with which to measure it"; it can also "easily feed into desires for authoritarianism, militarism, and nationalism, and can reinforce anxieties about racist and gendered connotations of waste."[16] The fact is, Daggett notes, "most visions of energy transition and fossil fuel divestment remain allied to the ideals of dynamism, efficiency and productivity." Consequently, "the obsession with counting, metering, and saving energy, and putting every unit to good use, ... have only become more urgent in an era of global warming."[17] We saw this "obsession with counting" and "metering" in Thunberg's #MindTheGap video. Advancing instead a postwork energy politics, which would deemphasize the subject supposed to know where and how to meter energy, Daggett shifts the focus to a "politics of pleasure," advocating, like Aronoff, "an insistence on work refusal and leisure."[18]

Without wanting to cast doubt on the political urgency of these postwork theses, which go a long way toward rethinking the pleasures of waste, I want to scratch at the anodyne image of sex that they put forth—that sex, unlike plastic or carbon pollution, is a redeemable kind of waste. The fact is, sex does put something to work, something that is incompatible with the pastoralized version of sex thrust on us by progressive critics.

What concerns me is the following: in a rush to valorize sex and analogize it with myriad other energy-saving activities, including leisure time, community, and self-care, sex, by which I mean the conceptual deadlock of sex (what is it?) and not any particular sexual act, has become less toxic—that is to say, less destructive to time, community, and self-care—than it properly should be. We have forgotten Leo Bersani's queer riposte—namely, the "refusal to prettify [sex], to romanticize it, to maintain that fucking has anything to do with community or love"—and so have covered over "the inestimable value of sex as," in Bersani's words, "anticommunal, antiegalitarian, antinurturing, antiloving."[19] No less polemical in her refusal to accept the pastoralized version of waste-free sex, Joan Copjec argues that "sex is the stumbling block of sense."[20] If sense or meaning binds untoward energy, be it erotic energy (bodily stimuli) or fossil energy (both are a form of crude energy), sex, in psychoanalysis, is the unbound, unknowable remainder of sense—thought's waste product. Sex is, consequently, excremental, not incremental; it does not add up to an increase of sense. Copjec asserts, "It is only there where discursive practices falter—and not at all where they succeed in producing meaning—that sex comes to be."[21] By pastoralizing sex, by making it analogous to other energy-saving activities, Aronoff and Daggett not only reinstate the subject supposed to know—here, the subject supposed to know what sex *is* and how it should be used—but also remove sex from the equation.

The stumbling block in both of these arguments and the problem I seek to address in these pages is that each call for a greener, happier, and more just world relies on metalanguage—on the image of a "subject supposed to know,"[22] a subject who has read the scientific data about the ice caps, deforestation, and climate feedback loops and is ready to act accordingly, with no gap. The problem is that, like the message in Thunberg's video, the environmental subject supposed to know is filled with gaps, loops, and unconscious wishes. The image of the gapless subject is just that, imaginary, because it sutures a subject riven by unconscious sexuality. The energy humanities begin with a subject misdirected by petro-ideology and try to reverse a negative interpellation. The problem is that the subject in reverse, diverted by ideology, is the only subject we know, the only subject we will ever know.[23] In Freud's account of the development of the ego, the latter emerges against a backdrop of libidinal waste. It is by splitting the self into two—between a subject supposed to know and an unconscious subject, the subject of the drives—that the ecological subject appears. Waste, in other words, is the (un)foundation of every environmentalism.

Contrary to the inconvenient truths espoused by ecologism—that capitalism is inimical to life, that the Arctic is vanishing, and that the current fossil economy is a vampire economy in which only the wealthiest survive—the real inconvenient truth is that *thought is hostile to life*. Thought cannot be recuperated in the service of the good, because thought only thinks in relation to waste—to the scraps or nothing-objects that Lacan, regarding sex, calls the Real. The Real isn't what lies beyond the gap (pace Thunberg); it is the gap itself.

As we will see in the environmental cinema of Kelly Reichardt, it is not by overcoming the fiction of capitalist ideology that we become gapless subjects; the fiction of the gapless subject is capitalist ideology at its peak. The way to a better energy economy, Reichardt's cinema shows, is not by citing the scientific doomsday reports or promising a happier, better tomorrow; this trope of ecological wholeness repeats the fiction of the capitalist $ubject. The way forward is not against the fiction but through it.

Thunberg's #MindTheGap video is representative of several strands of ecology, including Marxist, feminist, and decolonial ecology. By pointing to the gaps in our knowledge about the real, these discourses posit a socialist, feminist, and Indigenous subject *to come*.[24] They posit, in other words, a metalanguage: a subject who is outside the alienation of the signifier. That subject supposed to know is a gapless subject, said to stand outside the fictions of capitalist ideology. This subject supposed to know is now the implicit subject of environmentalism. To be sure, today's environmentalists (queer, posthuman, Indigenous, Marxist) posit a subject fully entangled with toxic environments. One will protest that these ecoentanglements do not afford such a pure outside and that the deconstructionist motto, "there is nothing outside of the text," applies to waste ecologies too.[25] And yet this version of ecodeconstruction maintains the subject supposed to know in a new guise. The toxified, "transcorporeal" subject[26]—the de facto subject of ecocriticism—is already *sanitized*, aspirationally attuned to its environment, confident in knowing its place in the world. Although we have grown confident in the notion that there is no outside and persist in saying we wear the world's pollution in the flesh, this meshed way of thinking nonetheless admits an intrusive outside that is the impossible Real. Otherwise, there would be no sense in denying the outside's disturbing force. Psychoanalysis calls this intrusive outside the unconscious.

The unconscious is our first and eternal waste product—far worse than plastics, pesticides, or plutonium, because it contaminates even our brightest visions of the future. Waste is, according to psychoanalysis, the bedrock of environmental thought. In Lacanian terms, it is the Real against which the ecological subject tries to purify itself. Both ecologism and green capitalism maintain a subject who—someday, in the future—will have it all without remainder. In the case of environmentalism, not only does this promise neglect the role of waste in stimulating desire (something that capitalism knows but keeps secret), but it also forbids desire at the same time. It is this unknowable energy remainder that falls outside the futural fantasy of fossil capitalism and the imaginary ego of the Green New Deal alike.[27] It is this intolerable remainder that, for example, energy scholars like Ashley Dawson cannot account for in their otherwise indisputable claims about sea level rise, warming, and the rapid extermination of species.[28] The gaps in subjectivity denounced by environmentalists are the direct result of the subject's constitutive relation to (sexual) waste. We cannot suture these gaps. The will to do so is part and parcel of the capitalist drive to overcome environmental and libidinal limits at any cost. Rather, it is the refusal of these gaps that drives environmental destruction today. It is not, in other words, the contradiction in thought between reality and fiction that stalls ecological progress; it is the fantasy of progressing beyond the contradiction that fuels the current conflagration. Ecofantasy is, consequently, a constipated fantasy; it does not know how to enjoy loss.

The Constipation of Ecology

Consider a passage from Freud on the subject supposed to know—that is, the subject on the pot:

> One of the clearest signs of subsequent eccentricity or nervousness is to be seen when a baby obstinately refuses to empty his bowels when he is put on the pot—that is, when his nurse wants him to—and holds back that function till he himself chooses to exercise it. He is naturally not concerned

with dirtying the bed, he is only anxious not to miss the subsidiary pleasure attached to defaecating. . . . The retention of the faecal mass, which is thus carried out intentionally by the child to begin with, in order to serve, as it were, as a masturbatory stimulus upon the anal zone or to be employed in his relation to the people looking after him, is also one of the roots of the constipation which is so common among neuropaths. Further, the whole significance of the anal zone is reflected in the fact that few neurotics are to be found without their special scatological practices, ceremonies, and so on, which they carefully keep secret.[29]

Confronted with the imperious demands of potty training, the infant, who is strictly conceived as pleasure-seeking, refuses the demands of the Other (the "nurse") and holds tight to its waste product, its feces. For the subject supposed to know, the contradiction of having and not having the satisfying object is unthinkable. In Aronoff's words, the preoedipal infant believes it can have nice things, without waste. Infantile constipation is, therefore, the psychoanalytic equivalent of the gapless subject; in both cases, action (fecal retention), awareness (conscious enjoyment), and time (no delay) come together. It is, consequently, a major achievement when, according to Freud, the infant eliminates its prized possession.

By eliminating a piece of itself as waste, the infant is one step closer to shaping a fictional ego (the me, or the subject supposed to know, versus the not-me, or the shit). The advent of the self in Freud's theory is primordially wasteful. Something must be sacrificed to produce the fiction of the self. The infant sacrifices oral, anal, and scopophilic enjoyment to become an imaginary ego in possession of its proper objects. Freud considers this an achievement not because the infant has given ground on its desire and conceded to the demands of the Other; on the contrary, the infant turns its prized object into shit when and only when it discovers the contradiction it enjoys—when, unconsciously, the subject learns that having and not having are one and the same. In Lacan's reading of Freud, we enjoy not the thing itself, the feces, but the lack in the thing, what it secretly stands in for. In other words, we enjoy the lack—the nothing—that the object gives. Through the fiction of the ego, our first proper object, the subject supposed to know lives in constant tension with waste—namely, the waste product that forms the unconscious. Libidinal waste—everything that is discarded from the imaginary ego—has a shelf life that far surpasses carbon dioxide. That is why Lacan calls the energy of the libido "indestructible life"[30]—it is the paradoxical, undead life of the drives. And yet these remnants of infantile enjoyment also point to a different energy economy beyond the fossil economy, one that I dare call sustainable, lasting, and renewable—even if it is hazardous to the self. The libidinal ecology of Freud's drive energy is the oldest renewable energy humanity has ever known, and yet it is not ours to use. The ethics of Freud's metapsychology entails renunciation, as outlined in a different theoretical register by Frédéric Neyrat.[31] Freud's energy requires renunciation of the subject supposed to know.

With the advent of unconscious enjoyment, pleasure is no longer a gapless, constipated pleasure, holding tight to its own certainty, but rather a laxative pleasure because the infant is free to explore other sources of enjoyment. By alienating a part of itself (the feces) to the Other, the subject supposed to know becomes a split subject. This subject is filled with gaps and loops in action, awareness, and time. Only by submitting to the fiction of the Other's demand do we learn to see the gaps in that fiction. Only by wasting a part of ourselves do we learn to enjoy the nothing that is presently absent in every object. In other words, through the Other's demand, we begin to see the contradictions in our own enjoyment. We can (not) have nice things.

Freud revisits the waste economics of potty training in a later essay, "Negation," in which he links the first eliminative act to the analytic setting. Freud writes, "The manner in which our patients bring forward their associations during the work of analysis gives us an opportunity for making some interesting observations."[32] When, for example, the patient says, "You ask who this person in the dream can be. It's *not* my mother,'" Freud translates: "So it *is* his mother."[33] What the patient believes to be the most "unlikely imaginable thing" (mental garbage) is, Freud argues, "the right admission."[34] The fictional "not" ("It's *not* my mother") produces the real gap in the statement—it is my mother. "Thus the content of a repressed image or idea can make its way into consciousness, on condition that it is *negated*," Freud argues. "Negation is a way of taking cognizance of what is repressed."[35] Put differently, negation is a way of living *with* waste. The greenist ideologues among us, the most energy-conscious, leftist, power-for-the-people activists, are, at bottom, wastrels, according to Freud. This means that no amount of consciousness-raising could possibly bring subjects to divest from waste. How could it? The very image we raise when we raise consciousness is the product of a wasteful negation; what is more, this image must go on wasting to maintain the fiction of a waste-free self. We cannot, then, appeal to a fictional entity (such as the waste-free subject) to overthrow the fiction of capitalist ideology, because the two are complicit. Capitalist ideology appeals to the imaginary ego's dream of having it all without remainder. What we need is not a realism of the activist subject but a realism of the unconscious.

As was the case in potty training, the patient turns a part of him- or herself into waste so that the illusion of a waste-free identity—the ego ideal—can continue. "I do not desire *x*" translates to "I desire x." The x is the subject's waste product—what it drops or discards in the sublimation of its own image. Freud describes this act of sublimation or negation as freeing, which could be construed as Freud's endorsement of the unitary, liberal subject, who is free to consume the world (without waste). However, this interpretation would be wrong. The real breakthrough of Freud's essay comes in the section on reality testing, in which Freud links freedom to waste. The latter is part and parcel of Freud's energoaesthetics. Freud writes, "The antithesis between subjective and objective does not exist from the first. It only comes into being from the fact that thinking possesses the capacity to bring before the mind once more something that has once been perceived, by reproducing it as a presentation without the external object having still to be there. The first and immediate aim, therefore, of reality-testing is, not to *find* an object in real perception which corresponds to the one presented, but to *refind* such an object, to convince oneself that it is still there."[36] Notably, the reality in question here is not pure, objective reality. The latter is already fully discarded by thought—by the mind's capacity to reproduce perception "as a presentation without the external object having still to be there." Freud's waste aesthetics is purely formalist. It reduces the vividness of the world to a formal outline or frame—images *without* content. The "without" in Freud's passage is crucial. For what this "without" means is something other than the constipation of thought, whereby, as in ecologism, thought gobbles up the world, leaving nothing in its wake. In fact, the opposite is true. Thought sacrifices itself by letting the world drop from the image—by becoming incontinent or contentless. Freedom, for Freud, doesn't mean having a lot of nice things; it means recognizing "nothing"—waste—as the kernel of the thing. Henceforth, refinding an object (such as the feces) is a purely formal endeavor; the task is "to convince oneself that it is still there." It is not. In Freud's theory, negation is integral to the thing. Something must be lost or negated so that "it" can be (re)discovered. Though we "convince" ourselves that the reality we see is "still there," the real, according to Freud, is already elsewhere—it is lost, dropped, or excreted in the very act of thinking it. To put this in aesthetic terms, we could say, after Jacques Rancière, that the distribution of the sensible precedes the sensible itself.[37] In less sanitary terms, we could say, after Freud, that thought shits itself into being. The object of knowledge, or love, is for all time thought raised to the level of the excremental Thing.

The mistake made by Freud's constipated subject was to assume that having the feces would make thought, action, and identity cohere. What Freud shows in "Negation" is that having the object, any object, is inherently foolhardy. Thought is always already emptied. But as psychoanalysis shows, thought can also think its own negation. Through analysis, thought encounters its unconscious attachment to waste, to everything that is no longer "still there." This is the freedom that Freud speaks of at the end of his essay. When we begin to see our desire as inherently wasteful, we can no longer be satisfied as constipated subjects. Instead of seeing behind the fiction of fossil capitalism, as environmentalism advocates, Freud prompts us to dwell in the space of an incontinent thought process, where there is no future to win, except the contentless future of an evacuated form.

Fidelity to the real, then, in Freud's sense, involves wasting time (and content). Paradoxically, it is through the delicate process of going nowhere, as in analysis, that the subject of the unconscious begins to surface. In contrast with the constipated subject of ecology—who insists that the real is just around the corner, that we can have nice things, and demands that we close the gap between knowledge and the real—the laxative subject whom I have been ex-plicating in these pages wastes time freely because the gap in knowledge, action, and time *is* the thing, the real that upsets our fictions, including our waste-free fictions.

Energosexuality

When enjoyment is tied to waste, politics loses its futural orientation and becomes Real in the Lacanian—and, I would argue, queer—sense. Brian Massumi offers an apt analysis of the real in his reading of the corporeal politics of Ronald Reagan. Before the Trumpocene, there was the Reaganocene. The former trumps the latter. Still, Reagan paved the way for Trump in more ways than one. Both presidents linked American identity and U.S. petrosupremacy to a hypermasculine ideal. But it wasn't just Reagan's imaginary appeal that accelerated the fossil economy. According to Massumi, what excited Reagan's followers wasn't just the tenor of his speech; it wasn't the rhetoric, oratory, or artfulness of his message—all of which were, in an important sense, lacking. What excited his listeners was the stupidity of the utterance—its gaps, jerks, and "cuts in continuity." "Reagan politicized the power of mime," Massumi argues. "That power is in interruption."

> A mime decomposes movement, cuts its continuity into a potentially infinite series of submovements punctuated by jerks. At each jerk, at each cut into the movement, the potential is there for the movement to veer off in another direction, to become a different movement. . . . In other words, each jerk is a critical point, a singular point, a bifurcation point. At that point, the mime almost imperceptibly intercalates a flash of virtuality into the actual movement underway. The genius of the mime is also the good fortune of the bad actor. Reagan's gestural idiocy had a mime effect. As did his verbal incoherence in the register of meaning. He was a communicative jerk.[38]

Reagan operationalized the gap in postmodern politics. He did so unwittingly. For the gaps in continuity that Massumi makes the site of "a critical point, a singular point, a bifurcation" in bodies and discourses are, strictly speaking, uncountable; the future they flash cannot be predicted or seen. Instead, they jerk forth like a jump cut in cinema. They are the unseen of body politics—unwilled, unanticipated, and so quickly sutured together by the media, whose job it is to quilt the nonsense together. A singularity is just that: a turning point, cut, or gap, which thought tries afterward to account for. But this is a losing effort. The veer does not interrupt a previous coherence. Reagan's "verbal incoherence" shows that politics is interrupted from the start. It begins not at 1 but at −1. The virtual is a negative value.

Fast-forward to the Trump era. "What is of dire interest now," Massumi argues, "post-Reagan, is the extent to which he [Reagan] contracted into his person operations that might be argued to be endemic to late-capitalist, image- and information-based economies."[39] Massumi foregrounds the haptic distraction (or "shock," as Walter Benjamin put it in the first half of the twentieth century) that accelerates today in the hypermediated, hypervisual, hyperglitch information economies of twenty-first-century, full-speed capitalism. "Think of the image/expression-events in which we bathe. Think interruption.... Think of the imagistic operation of the consumer object as turnover times decrease as fast as styles can be recycled. Everywhere the cut, the suspense—incipience."[40] Trump took the interruptive cut to a new level. The less his speech made sense, the more his supporters clamored to hear it. The master signifier of the Trump presidency was "America." But what made it a master signifier and Trump a buffoonish authoritarian was the gap that both embody. The emptiness of the master signifier and the incoherence of Trump excited voters by confronting them with their own lack. Consciously, they filled in the gaps in the president's speech by linking the signifier "America" with white nationalism. The latter quilted together the meaningless void in the president's incoherent speech. Unconsciously, however, it was the president's lack of full speech that triggered right-wing desire. Trump's incoherence opened a space of delay for desire to manifest. The space that Massumi calls "incipience," Trump rebranded as white power.

Although Massumi does not say so, his theory of the virtual, which he borrows from Gilles Deleuze, particularly the Deleuze of *Cinema 2*, owes a great deal to the psychoanalytic theory of the drive. Massumi's virtual cut echoes the virtual cut of the signifier, which leaves an uncountable remainder (gap) in language that can never be filled. This remainder inaugurates desire as the desire for that gap—for what is, essentially, objectless (the gap itself). Drive desire and conscious desire represent two different sides of sex. Whereas the latter is driven toward end pleasure and the extinction of excitation, drive satisfaction has no end. Or rather, the lack of an end is an end in itself. As subjects of the unconscious, we are driven to lose our objects again and again, and that—losing—is desire's true aim. Psychoanalysis is a loser's discourse. Yet it is also, for that reason, a critical energy discourse.

Psychoanalysis is first and foremost an "energopolitics," to use Dominic Boyer's apt term,[41] though he and the energy humanities have shied away from the energy politics of the drives in discussions of decarbonization. Sex, it would seem, lacks the high seriousness of solar panels and wind turbines. And yet Freudian metapsychology and the Lacanian rearticulation of drive energy as boundless, profitless expenditure that wastes the active subject by denying that subject the means-end delivery of libidinal profit is radically in line with the politics of decarbonization. The libidinal ecology of sex has this and only this to say to the carbon-intensive subject: divest! By wasting time with no end in sight, the drives divest from the market-driven demands of fossil capitalism. By occupying the somnambulant dream state of unconscious enjoyment, the drives show the subject a space outside the 24/7, carbon-intensive demand to lose sleep and, according to Jonathan Crary, extract profit.[42] Most of all, by learning to enjoy the dilatory time of the drives, the energy subject of psychoanalysis can begin to see beyond the horizon of settler-colonial time, variously theorized by Mark Rifkin, Nick Estes, and Macarena Gómez-Barris, where wastefulness is no longer the byproduct of capitalist accumulation but a goal in itself.[43] If, to the ecocidal ends of late carbon capitalism, the dilatory, self-satisfied, slow time of the drives is a waste to be uprooted at any cost, then an energy politics of the future must take up cause with the libidinal ecology of waste. This begins with a new understanding of the energy subject.

Unfortunately, this is not the direction the energy humanities have taken. Recent studies in the energy humanities have focused considerable attention on the history of energy waste and its resulting aesthetics. Many of these studies call for a fuller accounting of energy extraction, its uses and abuses, and for a redistribution of the sensible regarding how humans perceive—or fail to perceive—waste.[44] Curiously, virtually none of these studies engage closely with libidinal economy,[45] and this despite Allan Stoekl's pathbreaking work on sexual energy in *Bataille's Peak: Energy, Religion, and Postsustainability*. Neither does this work engage seriously with the vexed energy expenditures mapped by Freudian psychoanalysis and later reworked by Gilles Deleuze and Félix Guattari in *Anti-Oedipus*. There, sexual reproduction and discharge are counterposed to the repetitive, waste-driven ardor of the unconscious, where energy waste is endlessly recycled. In these examples, energopolitics has no unifying goal—neither ecologism's dream of zero-waste homeostasis nor capitalism's suicidal imperative to grow without limit. Both ideologies, energy conservation and energy profit, are rooted in a similar rejection of the queer energetics that Freud maps. For Freud, waste is inevitable. An energy complex itself, the ego is driven to expend energy profitlessly and at great subjective cost. Indeed, the repetition of waste is how the energetic subject *gets off*. Wasting time is, therefore, an inescapable energy imperative, one that directly conflicts with the temporal urgency of the activist subject.

This is where Kelly Reichardt's environmental cinema intervenes. Reichardt's fifth film, *Night Moves* (2013), about a group of radical environmentalists in Oregon, foregrounds the perilousness of energy extraction.[46] The bad object at its center is a hydroelectric dam. In twentieth-century environmentalism, dams became the primary object of environmental critique, despite their ambiguous status as renewable energy sources.[47] For the ecocentrist, whose philosophical mantra is Flow, Baby, Flow, the image of ecological blockage is an unbearable sight.[48] Dams do not emit greenhouse gases, but they do disrupt and destroy local habitats, endanger native species, and displace Indigenous communities. The decomposition of plant matter in dammed areas can also produce high levels of methane and carbon dioxide. The ecocentrists at the film's center see the dam not only as a limit to hydro flows but also as a limit to ecological freedom. Free the river, and you free your mind—this is the operating fantasy of ecocentrism, as witnessed by the film.

Night Moves takes a different view. It sees the limit—to action, knowledge, and ecological balance—as itself desirable and so scrutinizes the fantasy of a zero-waste future. In working to save the environment from external limits, the film's protagonists miss the psychic limits of any political project. They inflict damage in the name of preventing it.[49] By contrast, Reichardt's film, *as film*, doesn't just reject the speed of late capitalism; it injects cinema with the slow temporality and wasteful rhythms of unconscious enjoyment. These wasted spaces in the film's narrative are filled with dynamic tension, providing us, the spectators, a view of energy waste that is both asynchronous and antihuman. This version of energosexuality makes waste a necessary, albeit virtual, component of any reparative project—including the reparative work of film.

Sex in the Extractive Zone

Night Moves begins with a scene of blockage and release. A scene both tension filled and narratively empty, it begins on the site of one of Oregon's many hydroelectric dams. Reichardt's film visualizes pressure *release* (the conversion of the Columbia River into electric capital) while building visual *tension*. It is this contradiction between action release and repetitive energy buildup that characterizes much of Reichardt's environmental cinema. Focusing on the realism of Reichardt's ecocinema, Katherine Fusco and Nicole Seymour describe it as a cinema of "emergency," referring to the twin notions of *emergence* and *exigency* that define the sixth mass extinction, when slow environmental damage accelerates unpredictably, catastrophically.[50]

The film follows a group of environmentalists—Josh (Jesse Eisenberg), Dena (Dakota Fanning), and Harmon (Peter Sarsgaard)—who set out to blow up a hydroelectric dam in the name of saving lives. Provocatively, this plan (releasing the river to its natural thrust) fails. By blowing up the dam, these ecoradicals take a life—a camper sleeping downstream, whose body, washed away by the deluge, becomes the morbid rem(a)inder of the environmentalists' sweet-faced energopolitics. That remainder haunts the environmentalists with their own inadvertent waste product. Sure, they didn't mean to take a life. In Reichardt's film, however, unintentional damage is the point.

These environmentalists know facts. They cite the statistics on species collapse. They know the true ecoterrorists: corporate America, with its capitalist death cult, and economic growth. Josh speaks of "big" change: "It's got to be big. If people are going to start thinking anyway.... Killing all the salmon just so you can run your fucking iPod every second of your life. And that's what's gonna happen. People are gonna start thinking. They have to." Dena, in dialogue with Harmon, speaks of the imminent collapse of marine life:

DENA: In 2048, the oceans are gonna be empty.
HARMON: Yeah? Who says?
DENA: Science.
HARMON: Science? Maybe science is wrong.
DENA: No, 29% of edible fish have gone down by 90%. More people are moving to the coastlines, means more pollution, more waste. Situation is getting geometrically worse. It'll all go fast in the end. Once the marine biodiversity goes, everything goes with it.

These are the subjects supposed to know in Reichardt's film. Like other environmentalists in popular cinema—including the ecoterrorists of *12 Monkeys* (1995), the ecofascist Thanos in *Avengers: Endgame* (2019), and the time-traveling ecoactivists of *Tenet* (2020)—Reichardt's environmentalists are scientifically minded.[51] Nonetheless, they fail—and fail horribly.

The film's first shot opens on a giant pressure-release valve (figure 7), the kind used by hydroelectric dams to regulate energy flow. Josh, pensive, with hands gripped, gazes at the surge from above (figure 8). The blockage-release system (known in the trade as an impoundment dam) converts standing water into kinetic energy and kinetic energy into dollars. Hydroelectric dams not only extract value but also, Macarena Gómez-Barris argues, exact death. "Dammed landscapes are extractive zones," Gómez-Barris writes, "where military, corporate, and state technologies of

FIG. 7. Still from *Night Moves* (2013).

FIG. 8. Still from *Night Moves* (2013).

resource surveillance convert Indigenous and rural territories into a digital colony."[52] Considering the "exponential, if finite, social and ecological resources" required by large dams, Gómez-Barris asks, "what conceptual tools allow us to puncture the assumption of dispossession that is embedded in the logic of hydropower?" She offers a countervisual answer: "If we consider that the extractive viewpoint succeeds precisely by becoming the normative way we see and universalize the planetary, then . . .

Zero-Waste Sex   75

countervisuality reveals extractive zones as corporate and state collusion over the destruction of life, refocusing our attention upon a smaller scale of experience."[53]

While Reichardt's film does give us a variety of "smaller scale" countervisuals, the image it shows is not beneath or behind the extractive view but internal to it. Instead of replacing one substantive subject (the extractive subject) with another (the subject of submerged knowledge practices), Reichardt's film examines a zone *within* extraction: the zone of the drive.

Neither Gómez-Barris's submerged knowledge positions nor the ecocentrists' faith in vitalistic flows touches the real in Reichardt's film, because both are wedded to the gapless subject—Lacan's mythical subject supposed to know. As soon as Josh and Dena exit the dam, Dena exclaims, "Whoa. I think that was an oriole. I didn't know we had those." The bird is off camera, while Dena and Josh are squarely within the frame. Behind them, a sign reads, "Lake of the Woods." It includes a topological map of the wood, lake, and hydroelectric dam. Dena is amazed by the oriole; like the river and fish that she and Josh intend to set free, they imagine the bird's elusiveness, vitality, and motion as antithetical to the dam's destructiveness. The whole of *Night Moves* questions this antithesis. The ecocentrist's image of wild nature furthers, rather than explodes, the biopolitics of control that Josh and Dena see concretized in the dam, thus confirming Antoine Traisnel's argument about the biopolitics of capture. Traisnel shows that the technologies used to represent animal life for the purpose of studying and ideally preserving it, from the nineteenth century to now, instead further, rather than replace, the hunt. Traisnel's provocative application of the Foucauldian thesis that biopower extends the means of controlling life shows that "new aesthetic, scientific, and technological methods for pursuing live animals produced them as increasingly fleeting and endangered, making them all the more susceptible to new forms of biopolitical management."[54]

Recall Dena's enthusiasm for the unexpected and elusive oriole. According to Traisnel's panoptic thesis about the ruses of animal representation, eluding capture ensures the bird's eventual capture. And what is true for one animal, the oriole, goes for the human animal too. *Night Moves* maps obsessively the networks of surveillance and policing that govern life, including the wildlife of the Oregon forest. The ecoradicals—Josh, Dena, and Harmon—move from one form of capture to the next, despite their efforts to remain unseen. In this sense, *Night Moves* could be read as a Foucauldian nature flick, for it shows that the big Other, the prison, is everywhere.[55] There's no such thing as being "off the grid." At the end of *Night Moves*, Josh applies for a job at a sporting-goods store. The final image is of Josh looking up at a security mirror, his total visibility mirrored back to him (figures 9 and 10).

But just as the film rejects the anarcho-vitalism of its protagonists, so too it rejects the panoptic vision of total surveillance, as its most spectacular events take place off-screen. Traisnel is right to point out that the biopolitics of capture thrives on elusiveness and invisibility; when the dam explodes and the river is freed, what ought to be a celebratory event is registered in the film as a prolonged silence, punctuated by a muffled blast. The pressure-release system observed in the film's opening shot has been destroyed; the operation is a success. But the filmic pressure only builds. We see Josh, Dena, and Harmon pressed into the cab of a truck, the film's frame limning the windshield; the three stare forward, eyes ahead, and barely flinch at the sound of the exploded dam (figure 11). So quiet is the explosion that one could almost miss it. In contrast with the

FIG. 9. Still from *Night Moves* (2013).

FIG. 10. Still from *Night Moves* (2013).

FIG. 11. Still from *Night Moves* (2013).

freedom they intend through their actions, the three have never looked more confined. Although they are, from their perspective, driving forward from the scene of the crime, Reichardt's film puts the viewer in the position of Walter Benjamin's "angel of history," looking back at a "single catastrophe."[56] This is a staple of Reichardt's cinema. In *First Cow* (2019), for example, a character remarks, "History isn't here yet," referring to the nineteenth-century Oregon landscape. Against this version of historical predestination, akin to what Mark Rifkin calls "settler time,"[57] Reichardt herself turns the camera on those characters to reveal the ongoing catastrophe of that colonial mentality. Going forward in Reichardt's film feels like going nowhere. When Josh wakes the following morning, nothing has changed. The destruction of the dam grabs the media's attention, but the focus is not on "big" ideas. The focus is on the missing body, that obscene remainder that stains the environmentalists' progressive action. In Fusco and Seymour's analysis, the film thus "shows how unintended consequences go on the record, whether a criminal or a geologic one."[58]

To repeat, surveillance, the big Other, sees all. If this panoptic argument sounds reminiscent of my earlier claim that there is no metalanguage, it misses a crucial component: the unconscious. The energosexuality of the unconscious is itself an extractive zone (indeed, there are many such zones: oral, anal, visual, and auditory, to name a few). So while it is right to say there is no metalanguage and that Reichardt's film underscores this theoretical point, that does not mean that the Other (the network of biosurveillance) sees all. Quite the opposite, *Night Moves* insists on the opacity of desire, on a manner of wastefulness that lays waste to the subject supposed to know. It is this *other* real that concerns Reichardt's cinema. For a film that has almost nothing to show of sexual acts, it saturates the frame with a sexuality that is, to both the subject supposed to know *and* the subject surveilled, abyssal.

In yet another off-screen moment suggestive of the pleasures of free nature (the oriole; the river; at one point, Harmon interpolates the hydroelectric dam as a woman on the brink of sexual freedom: "God knows that dam wants to come down.... Everything in the world is telling her to give up and let go"), Josh hears Dena and Harmon having sex behind closed doors. Uninterested, he wanders into the nearby wood. The camera tracks his movement, ambling until he comes to a full stop. The day had been spent mixing ammonium nitrate fertilizer, the same agent used to accelerate crop growth, this time used as a lethal explosive. Stopping in the woods, Josh looks down at the palms of his hands (figure 12). Reichardt lingers there, as if silently performing a palmist reading of the lines etched on the surface of Josh's dirty skin. Concave, Josh's hands remain open for several seconds of quiet meditation. We linger in that dry, dermal landscape before cutting to the day of the explosion. Before that cut, there is tension but no release. A nearly identical scene of brooding wandering appears early on as an unnamed farmer addresses two others; he asks, "Where's Josh?" We learn Josh's name for the first time through that interrogative, but the name remains a placeholder—akin to the nickname/empty signifier of the previous chapter. Josh's character is impassive, moody—flat. Jesse Eisenberg achieves a quality of impersonality in Josh that is both smoldering and blank: smoke without a flame. Hence, the question "Where's Josh?" could also be read as an ontological question about the misinterpellation of the ecological subject, which barely registers in the film except as an instance of fading or *aphanisis*.[59] No sooner is Josh's absence called into question, however, than we see him. Stooped, crouching toward the ground, Josh cups a fallen bird's nest; again, his hands are empty, sky facing (figure 13). He

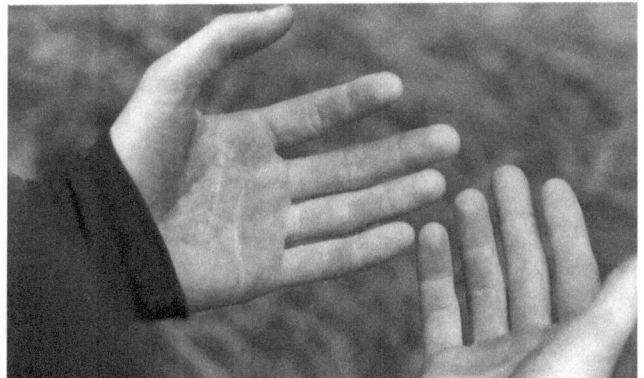

FIG. 12. Still from *Night Moves* (2013).

FIG. 13. Still from *Night Moves* (2013).

places the fragile nest on a branch. Seconds later, a woman in voice-over states, "The disaster we see is happening everywhere at the same time. The clock is ticking. It has been ticking for 150 years now, since the dawn of industrialization. We are a culture hooked on profit, production, and perpetual growth, but at what cost?" The voice-over and accompanying images of ecological destruction resemble Thunberg's #MindTheGap video. But Josh isn't listening.

These objects (hands and bird's nest) and the acts of tenderness he shows them are always private objects. Thus, our window onto them replicates the scopic regimes of surveillance that the film's protagonists work so hard to avoid. Though Josh would like to remain a question mark, he does enter the frame. What does *not* enter the scopic regime is the nothing-object that triggers Josh's desire. Both the concave of his hands and the hollow of the bird's nest echo the film's visual motif of rotational void objects, including the fertilizer mixer used to fabricate explosives, which the camera, detached from any forward movement, fastens on (figure 14). These objects—hands, nest, mixer, pressure-release valve—are waste objects from the perspective of the film's main action; in point of fact, they add nothing. That is the secret of their fetishistic pull or lag on the narrative. Visually proximate to the circuit of the drive, these rotational objects suggest—contra Josh, contra the #MindTheGap video's implacable environmental demand—that their manifestation of lack is what causes thought to think.

Of course, an ecological ethics of waste cannot refuse to act; to do so would be to render politics, including fantasy politics, which is what politics ultimately is in Reichardt's film, impossible. This book is not a call for political quietism, even if it does try to question certain environmental assumptions. Rather, an ecological ethics of waste begins by traversing the fantasy that thought produces the good, when, in fact, thought produces its opposite: waste. This is Lacan's point about the excrementality of sex. Sex is what falls away from the body of good sense; it not only causes the subject to act in his or her self-interest (this is the commonsense ecological argument that environmental action is in our best interest) but also—here is the hard part—*causes the subject*.

While the first cause happily goes about suturing every last gap in the ecological fabric, it misses the second, desultory

FIG. 14. Still from *Night Moves* (2013).

version of cause, which Lacan calls sex. Sex acts as a snag or tear in the ecological fabric, triggering the subject's curiosity with an ontological unknowable: sex—what is it? *Night Moves* shifts our focus away from the first cause, the destruction of a hydroelectric dam, to the second, unactionable cause: thought's destructiveness. Ultimately, it is this second cause, what I am calling energosexuality, that the film's environmentalists repress, with disastrous results.[60]

As spokespersons of the real, Josh, Dena, and Harmon confront the Lacanian Real in the corpus mortuum of irreparable loss. Saving leads to waste, but "leads to" oversimplifies the film's strange causality. Lacan writes that the unconscious is there where cause fails, where pressure release repeats an unassimilable remainder. *Night Moves* is interested in that other cause, the real of the unconscious, which takes pleasure in thwarting our best intentions. If minding the gap stands for good ecological sense, then it is safe to say that Josh, Dena, and Harmon mind the gap. My claim is that Reichardt's film minds that gap differently. Rather than filling it in with images of flowing rivers (we do not, in fact, as viewers, see the river in its pristine, undammed form after the detonation), the film insists on the gap's insuperable disturbance to ecological thought. That thought is stained by unconscious waste, which the film's obscene remainder, the floating corpse, reminds us of. Unwilling to wash that stain away, Reichardt's film challenges ecocriticism to begin *there*, where thought wastes itself.

4
The Lost D

The Youth Climate Strike, inspired by Greta Thunberg, and related movements, including Fridays for the Future and Extinction Rebellion, have gathered millions of activists worldwide to protest government inaction on climate change. The time to mitigate global warming is now, the youth activists argue. There is no planet B, the strikers contend. About this they are right.

Although there are plenty of reasons to be anxious about the future, Mari Ruti helps us linger on what is less evident in discussions about anxiety. The grip of anxiety is everywhere, Ruti observes. It is "the very air we breathe."[1] Ruti is not referring to climate anxiety, but her suggestion that anxiety constitutes an atmosphere—one that is inescapable—speaks to the greater concerns registered by climate activists. Many of us, probably all, deal with anxiety, but rarely do we consider anxiety worth sustaining. This, however, is what Ruti and others working in psychoanalytic criticism, including Todd McGowan, encourage us to do. Anxiety, they argue, is interminable; like it or not, *it stays*. Though it is clear there are exacerbating conditions that trigger anxiety, like overwork or lack of accessible childcare, housing, and prescription drugs, less clear is that our usual ways of dealing with anxiety may prolong anxious feelings. Rather than mitigate anxiety like carbon emissions, psychoanalysis teaches a counterintuitive practice of *sustaining* anxiety that could help combat the atmospheric pressure of our daily lives.

One way to sustain anxiety is to embrace what Ruti calls lack, after Lacan. Usually, we think of lack as antithetical to enjoyment. Eating or drinking excessively, chain-smoking, or binge-watching TV seems, on the surface, to have nothing to do with lack and everything to do with excess. Capitalist society places supreme value on excess and commands subjects to enjoy excessively at any cost, even if that cost is a habitable planet. An SUV, for example, is wildly excessive.[2] Most city dwellers do not need it, and its carbon emissions are exceedingly high. It is, therefore, an easy target of environmental criticism, which tends to preach modesty, conservation, and limits.

Rather than see excess and lack as antithetical and instead of countering excess with more excess (as green capitalists advocate), McGowan takes a dialectical approach to capitalist enjoyment and asserts that lack instigates our desire. If nothing were lacking, there would be nothing to desire and thus no impetus for excessive behavior. We enjoy excessively, McGowan argues, because deep down, lack is what we enjoy. Instead of separating excess and lack, McGowan suggests the true leftist act is to illustrate lack's libidinal appeal.[3]

My argument, following McGowan, Ruti, and others,[4] is that an anxiogenic climate such as ours requires a psychoanalytic intervention, one that Lacanian psychoanalysis is uniquely equipped to provide. Whereas the main currents of social critique, including Marxism, try to alleviate our social symptoms through visions of excess, offering a future satisfaction in contrast to our current dissatisfaction as anxious, overworked subjects, psychoanalysis maintains that the secret to our enjoyment is radically immanent. The psychoanalytic cure is ultimately deflationary, because it maintains that we are already satisfied at the level of the drive. Although we suffer terribly from bullshit jobs and feelings of alienation, such dissatisfaction aids the capitalist system, which promises an escape from dissatisfaction through the commodity. The standard leftist approach to dissatisfaction is not much different. Kate Soper, for instance, proffers an "alternative hedonism" as her version of the good life in a postscarcity, postcapitalist world, where dissatisfaction has been overcome. Although no one on the Left would dispute the need for a way out of capitalist immiseration, the psychoanalytic path to a postscarcity world is one that recognizes that we are already satisfied. After Freud's discovery of the death drive, which satisfies itself on absence, the psychoanalytic cure undergoes a dramatic transformation. The goal is no longer to overcome dissatisfaction—that would be a bonus—but to change one's life on the basis of the drive's present satisfaction. We enjoy, in other words, not despite the symptom but through it. We enjoy the lack that anxiety and vexation give. The path to a postcapitalist world begins with the recognition that we are already satisfied. A satisfied subject of the drive has no interest in accumulating a lot of things and thus no interest in sustaining the capitalist order.

Waiting for the Phallus

One of the clearest examples of Lacan's thesis on anxiety comes from the film *The Lost City* (2022), starring Sandra Bullock, Channing Tatum, and Brad Pitt.[5] Bullock plays Loretta Sage, a romance novelist who would rather be writing serious scholarship and feels, despite her popularity, that she has not lived up to her potential as a writer. Tatum stars as Alan Caprison, a wannabe romantic hero. He is the face, chiseled torso, and persona printed on the cover of Sage's best-selling romance-adventure series and its most recent novel, *The Lost City of D*. Despite Caprison's cover-model good looks, he is only a "want-to-be" in Lacan's sense of *manque-à-être*, because he lacks the being of the phallic hero imagined in the novels. Put simply, Tatum's character lacks the D.

When the fictional universe of *The Lost City of D* becomes a reality and the plot turns to finding the lost D (the twenty-first century's comic answer to "The Purloined Letter"), Sage and Caprison embark on an adventure that they are ludicrously unfit to accomplish. Enter Brad Pitt as Jack Trainer. Trainer plays the phallic hero—the real-life embodiment of the fictional hero of the *Lost City of D*. He fights, he wins, and he does not fear danger. He has the D. Until he doesn't.

The Lost City proves its cinematic greatness by killing the phallic hero swiftly and unceremoniously. After Trainer is shot dead, the film and its characters go on without the phallus to protect them. The film's plot is of little importance compared to the castration anxiety that it inflicts on viewers (who were expecting to see Brad Pitt) and the characters in search of the lost D. The D does not come, and that is the film's message. *The Lost City* combines the excess of the romance genre with the lack that most films, especially romance films, try filling before the final credits. Instead, *The Lost City* invites viewers to find humor in the anxiety-inducing lack that the lost D represents.

Of course, phallic authority takes on many different guises in capitalist society, not all of them as obvious (or funny) as Pitt's character in *The Lost City*. Donald Trump is an obvious example of right-wing phallic authority, yet the reach of phallic power is widespread. It can include girlbosses, men with man buns, environmentalists, and woke liberals. Indeed, one of the possibilities imagined by *The Lost City* is that we have entered a new phallic order, in which the old phallus (represented by Pitt) has been replaced by a newer, softer phallus (represented by Channing Tatum). Hard or soft, the phallus has one function: to conceal the lack in the Other, either by externalizing it, minimizing its visibility, or both.

Figures like Jack Trainer in *The Lost City* or Trump in real life occupy the role of the big Other, the figure of social authority in Lacan's theory, by convincing desiring subjects that their desire has an answer and that answer is accumulation. By accumulating a lot of things, we can, the big Other tells us, overcome the trauma of castration. Consequently, capitalist subjects search for objects that will satisfy not only their desire but the Other's desire as well—objects, that is, with the power to confer the Other's recognition and approval. For example, I desire the new job or the new commodity not because of its intrinsic value but because I believe unconsciously that it is what the Other (the parent, the life coach, the social media influencer) wants from me and what the Other also wants. These two forms of desire are the same in Lacan's theory—the subject's desire is the desire of the Other. In this way, the Other outfits capitalist subjects with a fantasy of fulfillment while obscuring the trauma of their enjoyment—an enjoyment that they already obtain through loss.

The Lost City is largely a response to psychoanalysis's baseline question of subjectivity: What does the Other (the figure of social authority) want from me? The film tells us. The Other wants the D.

However, assuming the position of the phallus proves difficult. In Lacan's view, what is mistakenly called "frustration anxiety" in object-relations psychoanalysis is not the frustration of a need but the frustration of a lack that no object can fill. Whereas a need such as hunger can be satisfied with food, desire is of a different order, the order of the signifier, which introduces lack into the subject's universe. Lacan calls this primordial lack *objet a*. Instead of conferring wholeness to the subject who seeks it, the *objet a* causes the subject to want what is, for lack of a better word, missing—a hole. The phallus is a substitution, a veil concealing the lack that confounds subjectivity. As such, it has no substance of its own.

A great deal of ink has been spilled propping up the Lacanian phallus and chopping it down. But the point of the Lacanian phallus is that it is already divided. The phallus is an empty signifier—the empty signifier par excellence. Unable to possess the *objet a*, the kernel of the Other's desire, the subject disavows castration through substitution. I cannot solve the Other's desire, but I can have the new car, job, or house. Lacan calls this act of substitution "phallic jouissance." It is the pittance of enjoyment given to us by the symbolic order, which, importantly, *enjoys in our stead*. Phallic jouissance is the jouissance of the "want-to-be" (*manque-à-être*), according to Lacan, who believes that he has solved the mystery of the Other's desire, that he wields phallic authority, and that there is, in fact, more to the phallus than meets the eye.[6] There's not. Phallic jouissance obscures the trauma of enjoyment, the enjoyment of lack, to be specific, by casting that enjoyment onto outsiders. It is, therefore, the paradigm of right-wing enjoyment, as we shall see next.

Between Two Anxieties

The popular television show *Yellowstone* (2018–24), an update on the western genre that stars Kevin Costner, gives a compelling image of phallic jouissance as it attempts to mask the anxiety at its core.[7] The show indulges in the lasting myths of white settler colonialism, featuring a ranching family in Montana, the Duttons, beset by the encroachment of real estate developers, a Native American casino, and the castrating power of global capitalism with its terrifying symbols of detumescence—that is, high-end boutiques slinging faux-Indigenous wears, pour-over coffee, and stuffy wine bars—all of which contribute to the castration anxiety suffered by the Duttons. The embodiment of white phallic power in America, the Duttons are Christian, God fearing, gun toting, violent, and hell-bent on preserving the family. The patriarch, John Dutton (Kevin Costner), is the show's center of phallic authority. As the show's big Other, he divides the world between family and foe and wields excessive violence to maintain the privileges of the Dutton name. His children fear and love him; they fear his retribution even as they love and idealize the image of strength, ruggedness, and authenticity he upholds. To his children and most others, he is the sovereign exception, both in and outside the law.

Although his children live in fear of what their father, the phallic Other, wants and spend their lives trying to fulfill their father's impossible demands, they enjoy the barrier that the Dutton name erects. This barrier or limit is epitomized by the ranch, an emblem of Dutton identity and its contested boundaries.

The phallic figure not only creates a mythic inside for those who pledge allegiance to the Dutton family name, some of whom literally wear a brand, but also produces an outside that his followers can enjoy through exclusion. In this way, the phallic father divides the structure of anxiety: between a menacing and castrating "other" (everyone who wants to steal the Duttons' phallic enjoyment) and a protective, if no less frightening, big Other, who demands loyalty in exchange for inclusion (John Dutton himself). By projecting the threat of castration onto others, the phallic father can wrap himself in the illusion of paternal care and offer coherence against a menacing outside.

But this external "other" beyond the border of the Dutton estate masks a far greater problem with phallic authority that the show exposes. The phallic father is already lacking. John Dutton, we learn, has cancer, and he fears his days are numbered. Although he cares for his family's land, his business (cattle ranching) is destructive to the land and the endangered species inhabiting it. He claims to do everything (bribery, blackmail, intimidation, murder) for his family, but no clear successor is willing to inherit and preserve the family estate. Lastly, he paints himself as a defender of American identity, even though his and his family's identities derive from stolen Indigenous land. This apparent contradiction is not a problem for the show. In one episode, after a particularly harrowing series of attacks on the white settler family, Dutton's Indigenous daughter-in-law turns to him and says, "You're the Indian now."[8]

The father in *Yellowstone* is the perfect example of phallic enjoyment. Although he appears to have so much, his power is empty, fraudulent. The show exposes the phallic imposture as just that, illusory. Beyond cowboy hats, chaps, guns, and whiskey, the thing that defines phallic power on the show is exclusion. As an impossible masculine ideal, the phallic figure cannot be a signifier among other signifiers but must stay concealed, hidden behind cowboy hats and belt buckles, for phallic authority to work. Furthermore, to the extent that we, the viewers, want this phallic authority to work, it is because we sense that something is missing from the Other—a trauma insofar as the Other's desire is our own. We sense an echo of our own lack in the phallic imposture, the anxiety of which is too great.

The Lack of Lack, or Worse

This anxiety-inducing situation becomes far more acceptable, however, when the threat of castration is projected elsewhere. By projecting the threat of castration onto an external other, the excessive presence of the Other becomes bearable, even desirable. Yes, I am discomfited by the excessive presence of the Other about whom I would like to know (*What do they want from me?*), and yet I prefer this excessive presence to the lack embodied by those whom the Other excludes.

According to Lacan, the structure of anxiety contains both poles: excess on the one hand and lack on the other. I am anxious before the Other, first and foremost, because the Other is lacking and so am I and, second, because the Other demands something of me that I would like to give and be—namely, the phallus. The genius of *Yellowstone* is that it splits the structure of anxiety so that excess and lack stand in opposite corners. It shows the falsity of that opposition and the racial, genocidal, and environmental violence that stems from treating anxiety as external.

Arguably, this is the fundamental trick of our anxiety-fueled capitalist age. Although we work and work anxiously, driven by the question "What does the Other (the boss, the stock market, parents, professors, police, social media, dating apps, the wellness industry) want from me?" most would prefer this form of anxiety to the threat of castration. In other words, capitalism's staying power results from the fact that it tricks people into seeing excess (power, pleasure, wealth) as separate from lack.[9] If (as the story goes) we could simply figure out how to make the boss happy; invest properly; be a better partner or lover; and live a happier, healthier, sexually fulfilled life in accordance with nature, *then*, we imagine, anxiety will abate. Capitalist anxiety is excessive because it fuels endless searching for phallic mastery—a phallic mastery that does not exist. The Left does a version of this. While it is true that the leftists promising "luxury communism" or the Green New Deal are doing so against the capitalist system, the utopias they imagine (technofuturist or green) are already infected by capitalist thinking; they focus on dissatisfaction instead of the satisfaction that comes from lack.

Compare capitalist anxiety to its supposed opposite, and we start to see how capitalism depends on the very figures of lack it excludes. In *Yellowstone*, dispossession by white settler colonialism makes Indigeneity a perfect symbol of the threat of castration. Capitalism depends on excluded figures like the Indigenous subject in *Yellowstone* to give coherence to the excessive demands of the phallus. By externalizing lack, capitalism masks its internal contradictions (the fact that, as an anxiety-producing structure, it is both excessive and lacking). Without the excluded other, vividly portrayed in *Yellowstone* by the border of the Dutton ranch, capitalism would cease to function. It would cease to function because it could no longer promise a way out of anxiety.

Capitalism promises an escape from anxiety while confronting capitalist subjects with something equally if not more anxiety provoking: the obscene excess of capitalist authority. Donald Trump can fill the White House with McDonald's burgers, support white nationalists and domestic terrorism, enrich his private interests using the office of the presidency, abuse women, disparage journalists, bully the disabled, and build golf courses in vulnerable areas of the planet while dismantling basic environmental protections. Yet he can still garner the love of his followers, because he pins their lack on others: immigrants, Black Lives Matter protestors, antifascists, and so on—subjects who, according to Trump, enjoy excessively and want to steal his supporters' enjoyment too.

Splitting the structure of anxiety into two external positions (one aspirational, the other threatening) is the greatest trick performed by capitalist society, and it explains the inextricable bond between capitalism and racism. The worst nightmare for racial capitalism would be if these external positions, excess and lack, came together. Of course, they do; dialectically speaking, they are never separate. Lack fuels excessive desire, and desire desires what is unobtainable in the Other. Nevertheless, much ideological work goes toward keeping these dialectical poles separate.

We are thus left with a choice between two different anxieties (one lacking, the other excessive) or a third, worse anxiety that is interminable and corrosive to the capitalist system. That interminable anxiety, from Freud's essay "Analysis Terminable and Interminable" to Lacan's *Seminar* X, is a stumbling block to subjects (all subjects) divided between excess and lack.

What the Multiple Misses

Crucial to note, however, is that, when it comes to anxiety, theory stumbles too. Insisting on figures of multiplicity (entanglement, assemblage, mesh) over and against the tyranny of the One, radical theory (from Foucauldian desubjectification techniques to Derridean *différance*) offers numerous ways to escape the anxiety-producing demands of the Other.[10] Yet it also repeats the split structure of anxiety. It relegates lack elsewhere, allowing the Other, who appears to have all the power, to occupy the master's position. Multiplicity theory places itself in a reactionary role, endlessly deconstructing the very thing it depends on to give it its radical guise.

The popular film *Toy Story* (1995) articulates what is most at stake in the turn to the multiple in radical theory: "To infinity and beyond."[11] This quixotic catchphrase, uttered by Buzz Lightyear, stands in stark contrast to *Toy Story*'s other phallic hero, Woody. In Western phallogocentric culture, has there ever been a better, more emblematic name for phallic mastery than "Woody"? Looking at this arborescent figure, it seems clear that Buzz's intoxicating name and embrace of the multiple makes him a preferable *Nom du père* for theory. If Badiou's *Being and Event* were a toy, it would be Buzz Lightyear.[12]

Still, history is not always kind to theory, and this is true of the multiple also. Consider an example: On June 14, 2022, Patricia Heaton, costar of the American TV show *Everybody Loves Raymond*, tweeted her outrage about Disney/Pixar's decision to drop Tim Allen (of *Home Improvement* fame) as the voice of the new Buzz Lightyear, asking, "Why would they completely castrate this iconic, beloved character?"[13] The reason for Heaton's objection is not immediately obvious. As the comment thread to Heaton's post points out, the new Buzz Lightyear, helmed by Chris Evans, is a cartoon ode to the masculine ideal—a far cry from Heaton's castrated Tool Man. He is cut, the commentators argued, but not *that* kind of cut.

Nevertheless, Heaton's tweet raises a valid point about the direction of the new Buzz Lightyear, even if her concern is couched in conservative gender ideology. The new Buzz is chiseled. The question keeping many of us up at night—is Buzz bald under that purple space cap (baldness being a common symbol of castration)?—is answered: *he is not*. Arguably, the new Buzz Lightyear dramatizes the concern registered by Heaton's tweet—that the figure of multiplicity is least equipped to accept castration and would rather go to outer space than reckon with it. Just look at Jeff Bezos.

Although the multiple seems like the most radical position that one could adopt against phallic authority, the multiple mirrors and so legitimizes that same authority. The multiple promises *more*—more newness, more surprise, more pleasure—and thus delays the subject's traumatic encounter with lack. McGowan points out that even a thinker of radical absence like Jacques Derrida still holds on to the promise of the *to come*—thus minimizing the threat of castration.[14] Derrida's specters are always promising more on the horizon. In this way, the multiple echoes the metonymic structure of capitalism, promising subjects the opportunity to enjoy without limits. What the multiple misses, however, is that subjects *only* enjoy when there are limits—when, in other words, lack and excess combine. Buzz Lightyear is a comic instance of the multiple repeating the phallic pursuit of *more*. Yet he also highlights a pervasive trend in contemporary theory.

Eugenie Brinkema's *Life-Destroying Diagrams* represents the high point of multiplicity theory today. Reading *Life-Destroying Diagrams*, one may be titillated, surprised, or more likely frightened by the dizzying array of epigraphs, ornaments, creative typography, stage directions, parentheticals, lists, and negative space, which scream from the page, "READER, BEWARE." Yet within this unfolding multiplicity, a thread runs through the labyrinth connecting essential points. The thesis? It is an avowedly Heideggerian one—form has been forgotten.[15] Brinkema challenges the ossification of thought as bone, spinal column, and "neck"—her metaphor for the horror critic's obsession with upright, cervical meanings like those derived from history or etymology. What, you might ask, is horror according to the horror critic? Brinkema tells us. It is the shuddering body, the threat of otherness, the cadaver of history lurching forward. Such readings—in turn biological, ethical, political, and historical—serve as stubborn supports for the forgetting of form and so lose everything, Brinkema argues—everything but the neck.[16] "Neck essentialism" converts form into allegory; it is, to adjust our terms, lacking, whereas the multiple of radical formalism is excessive, luxuriant, and *new*.[17] Sorry, but if you go to horror films to feel tingles down your spine, you have been duped, Brinkema argues. In fact, we all have, just about. Even the most Deleuzian among us sacrifices the luxurious nonsense of form for a series of mundane "me" statements like "It thrilled me" or "It shocked me." In so many ways, then, theory betrays its speculative calling. Like Heidegger, whose philosophical demolition begins with forgetting ("[The question of Being] has today been forgotten," Heidegger writes in *Being and Time*),[18] Brinkema breaks our present-at-hand concepts to unleash the radicality of the unready-to-hand: forms not obfuscated by use. Radical formalism breaks form from function and severs head from neck. Break the neck, Brinkema argues, and we break the slumber of theory. What else is a neck good for, except for breaking?

Though Brinkema's goal in *Life-Destroying Diagrams* is to

return thought to its speculative foundation, on this matter, the question of the neck, there is no room to speculate—the neck is good for nothing and has nothing to say. It is dumb. Let's stop talking about it.

A thinker more interested in the idiocy of the everyday, G. W. F. Hegel would disagree. Though Hegel does not theorize the neck per se, he does theorize the bone, that ossified column that supports our necklike propositions. Hegel writes, "The *being of Spirit is a bone*."[19] Read dialectically, Hegel's statement cuts in two directions. Spirit is mediated by bone, alienated by it, *and*, importantly, there is something of bone in Spirit. Hegel fractures the cervical column—it is and is not mere bone. But he also fractures Spirit—it is and is not Spirit. In Hegel's dialectic, both sides (Spirit and bone) fail to escape the obfuscation that Heidegger attributes to the tool. Even our dumbest, most forgetful, present-at-hand activities contain a kernel of truth in Hegel's philosophy. Dumb affect is not a mistake of theory; for Hegel, there are *only* mistakes. Consequently, theory succeeds not by cutting its enemy's throat but by cutting its own throat. Only losers win in Hegel's philosophy.

At an eventful moment in *Life-Destroying Diagrams*, Brinkema offers arguably the starkest formal account of multiplicity in the language of universal quantifiers. Although it is the same formal language Lacan deploys in *Seminar* XX, Lacan is nowhere cited.[20] This observation is of more than bibliographic interest; according to Brinkema, no one (not me, not you, no one in the history of humanity) escapes death's design, a truism Brinkema represents with the symbol $\forall x$. Death comes for all ($\forall$). Although this seems inordinately obvious, Brinkema's point is that being-toward-death gives life (and film) structure. The very structure of life is being-toward-death. Its eventuality is immanent, its scythe ever at our tender necks.

But there is an exception to the ∀x, at least one who is not subject to death, who escapes it. Brinkema uses the existential quantifier ∃x to represent the exception to the rule. To be clear, the exception is a lie; it is a fantasy. Yet the fantasy of the ∃x persists. Heidegger's whole philosophy is a meditation on the persistence of the ∃x—that is, on the forgetting of Dasein's authentic temporal existence. Likewise, Derrida's grammatology reveals the repressed being-toward-death of writing. And Giorgio Agamben lays bare the ∃x as the sovereign exception.

Although there is no exception to radical formalism, there is the recalcitrant, bony neck of theory, symbolized by the ∃x; that neck is, unfortunately, broad. It includes affect theorists, phenomenologists, object-oriented ontologists, film scholars, philologists, philosophers, psychoanalysts, Marxists, historicists, ecocritics . . . The list goes on. I will spare you the ignominy of your inclusion. After all, the confederacy of dunces in Brinkema's book is widespread, and we are all in it. The brilliance of Brinkema's book is to show the absurdity of the exception. For *there is no exception* in Brinkema's argument. No one escapes formalism's cut.

But there is a key difference between Brinkema's radical formalism, illustrated by the universal quantifiers ∀x and ∃x, and Lacan's. For Lacan, death is of little importance. The unconscious knows nothing of it, is unconcerned with Dasein and our original temporal thrownness. The unconscious knows no seasons. Instead, it is castration that the "all" of ∀x symbolizes in Lacan's mathematical formula. While it is true that death frightens, only castration cleaves the subject from himself, constituting a much more disturbing (and lasting) cut than death.[21]

The upshot of radical formalism is clear—it gives the reader freedom of thought without object, commodity, or utility. Oddly, this life-destroying formalism gives *life* to theory. By contrast, the neck and all it metaphorizes is ossifying, impossibilizing, restrictive, and deadening, a mere fossil of radical form—form with a boring necktie.

Multiplicity theory promises *everything*, yet it retrenches a basic dualism, opposing itself to Others who become bigger and more anxiogenic as a result. The radical formalist position sustains the anxiety-inducing Other, because there would be nothing to deconstruct or multiply without the Other's imposture. Consequently, theory feeds and destroys the very thing it opposes.

It is not clear, then, that the turn to multiplicity moves the dial toward radicality. After all, who cares about multiplicity when multiplicity is all there is? As Alain Badiou argues, the infinity of differences isn't extraordinary; it is a banal fact of existence.[22] Difference alone does not ensure the event. Instead, it keeps the structure of anxiety firmly in place by opposing excess and lack.

Left Enjoyment

No film better captures the misery of the multiple than *Everything Everywhere All at Once* (2022). The film pretends to celebrate the multiple by taking the multiverse as its narrative conceit. But it takes the multiverse *on* by critiquing the multiple as a reactionary and doomed political and aesthetic response to anxiety.

The film centers on a Chinese American family living in California. They are the real-world embodiments of the multiverse: multilingual, multigenerational, multicultural, and multiply divided by their competing dreams and aspirations. They run a failing laundromat. The mother, wife, and daughter of the family, Evelyn Wang (Michelle Yeoh), is overwhelmed by anxious feelings about her father's excessive expectations, an audit on the family business, and her perceived lack of success. Meanwhile, her husband, Waymond Wang (Ke Huy Quan), is planning to divorce her, and her daughter, Joy Wang (Stephanie Hsu)—anxious about her mother's demands to be thinner, more successful, and less queer—is slipping toward the only thing she has left: nihilism.

When Evelyn, the film's unlikely hero, enters the multiverse, it all sounds eerily familiar. Her contact from afar, the intergalactic multiple of Waymond, nicknamed Alpha Waymond, explains to Evelyn what is at stake: "I know you have a lot of things on your mind, but nothing can matter more than ... the fate of every single world of our infinite multiverse."[23] Alpha Waymond explains the situation like a would-be Peter Sloterdijk. He speaks of bubbles: "This is your universe, one bubble floating in the cosmic foam of existence. Every surrounding bubble has slight variations. But the further away you get from your universe, the bigger the differences." This differential foam would not be a problem if not for the sudden sliding occurring throughout the multiverse, brought about by the film's villain, Jobu Tupaki, who we learn is Evelyn's daughter, Joy. "She's been building something," Alpha Waymond laments.

ALPHA WAYMOND: We thought it was some sort of black hole.... We don't know what exactly it is. We don't know what it's for. But we can all feel it. You've been feeling it too, haven't you? Something is off. Your clothes never wear as well the next day, your hair never falls in quite the same way, even your coffee tastes wrong. Our institutions are crumbling, nobody trusts their neighbor anymore, and you stay up at night wondering to yourself ...

EVELYN: How can we get back?

Alpha Waymond's description of the multiverse as a chaotic system in which "institutions are crumbling, nobody trusts their neighbor," and no one can sleep at night sounds a lot like the anxiety-laden conditions of present-day capitalism.

Less obvious, perhaps, is that it's also a pretty good description of a wide range of theory, from Bergsonian *élan vital* to Butlerian performativity, insofar as nothing in these theories truly repeats—nothing "falls in quite the same way"—except multiplicity. The brilliance of *Everything Everywhere* is that it treats this unending multiple as the anxiogenic condition of our time. Though the multiverse in lesser films saves the day by deconstructing the mendacity of the One, the turn to fragmented multiples repeats rather than ruptures the problem of anxiety, leaving us one of two bad choices: appease the demands of the Other or resort to cynicism.

Joy takes up the latter position. "Commanding the infinite knowledge and power of the multiverse," the film's version of a Twitter account, Joy has "seen too much" and "lost any sense of morality, any belief in objective truth." When Joy reveals her master plan to her mother, Evelyn is surprised to learn that there is no plan—no black hole, no Death Star, only boredom.

JOY: I got bored one day, and I put everything on a bagel. Everything. All my hopes and dreams, my old report cards, every breed of dog, every last personal ad on Craigslist. Sesame. Poppy seed. Salt. And it collapsed in on itself. 'Cause you see, when you really put everything on a bagel, it becomes this. The truth.
EVELYN: What is the truth?
JOY: Nothing matters.

Joy is the film's radical formalist. She puts everything on a bagel, the sphincteric form of the universe, only to show the nothing at its center (figure 15). Joy tears down the obfuscations of the world. There are no anchors, no quilting points in Joy's multiverse, only the infinite plurality of forms.

Everything Everywhere is unique among multiverse films because it is critical of the multiverse concept. Pitting Evelyn

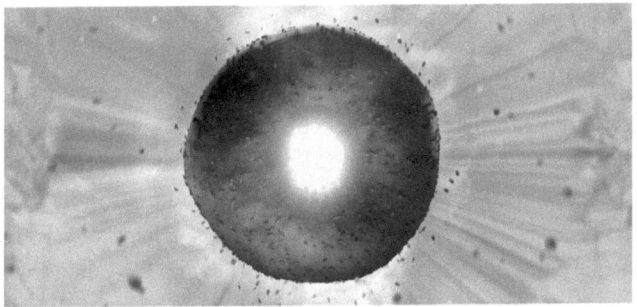

FIG. 15. Still from *Everything Everywhere All at Once* (2022).

(the impossibly demanding Other) and Joy (the teenage cynic) against each other, the film shows that the two positions are structurally interdependent and mutually reinforcing. The multiverse does not relieve the anxiogenic demands of capitalism (remember, Evelyn, too, has big Others in her life, including her father and the IRS); it intensifies them. As Alpha Waymond states, "We can all feel it," the multiple without anchorage. "You've been feeling it too, haven't you?"

McGowan argues that comedy is the one genre that brings excess and lack together.[24] *Everything Everywhere* is a good comedy for that reason. Though everyone in the film feels a sense of lack and believes that life's excess is enjoyed elsewhere (in romance films, in other universes), it ends by dialectizing excess and lack. Much like other heroic archetypes (Luke Skywalker in *Star Wars* and Neo in *The Matrix*), Evelyn lives up to her promise by mastering the multiverse and becoming a powerful wielder of *différance*. However, this proves a losing battle against an enemy, her daughter, who, like your average capitalist, believes in nothing but the proliferation and psychoticization of the multiple. They exchange blows, but nothing changes. True change only happens when Evelyn stops being multiple and accepts the deadlock of her subjectivity. By rejecting the

The Lost D 103

multiverse, Evelyn gains access to the one affect that does not deceive: anxiety.

Near the film's final sequence, Evelyn recognizes that an infinite array of universes is no match for the sweet imbecility of her husband, Waymond. Waymond acknowledges his shortcomings but explains that what others perceive as weakness (his lack of phallic mastery) is his strength, his means of survival. Waymond enjoys the constitutive anxiety that Lacan and Ruti align with the subject's internal division. In other words, Waymond brings lack (castration) and excess (enjoyment, jouissance) together. What had seemed like a deficit on the part of her husband, a lack needing to be filled, Evelyn reimagines as a vehicle of radical transformation.

Evelyn stops fighting like a reactionary. Instead, she upholds her constitutive anxiety—a sign of her inner division—showing her daughter that is who Evelyn is. An echo of Freud's famous *"Wo Es war, soll Ich werden"* ("Where the id was, the ego shall be"), Evelyn acknowledges what she could not acknowledge before (her failings as a mother) and, as a result, finds relief from the exhausting demands of the Other and the reactionary demands of the multiverse. Anxiety brings her to this discovery, signaling the lack that had fueled her excessive striving and obstinance toward her daughter. The film's true radicality occurs at this moment, not in the sliding of the multiverse, not in Joy's refusal to anchor in the here and now, but in Evelyn's decision to bring excess and lack together before her daughter.

A subject riven by lack may look to the Other to complete them, but this is a losing strategy. The strength of *Everything Everywhere*'s ending and what makes it a leftist film is that Evelyn and Joy find a common cause in each other's destitution. Instead of fleeing their constitutive anxiety, either in the Other or the multiverse, they embrace it by embracing each other. Although leftist theory rejects the big Other and does so in defense of those who are lacking, it could, following Evelyn, learn to make lack part of its political agenda.

This is not an easy task for leftist organizing, yet its implications for leftist thinking are profound. What would the Green New Deal look and sound like if it rallied for lack instead of excess? The tendency on the Left is to promise more—more happiness, more downtime, more luxury, more sex.[25] These are vital concerns because they bear on the Left's commitment to freedom and equality. However, the promise of *more* cleaves lack from the equation. A similar antinomy appears in the rhetoric of the youth climate strike—not only its emblematic figure, Greta Thunberg, but also its rhetoric of futurity, which dovetails with a morbid strain in queer theory, metaphorized by Lee Edelman as the figure of the child.[26] The youth climate strike movement insists on the future, understandably so. But a strike *for* the future echoes rhetorically the very thing that the climate strikers attack. Fossil capitalism is also a futural form; its inner child demands endless growth.

Admittedly, lack is a hard term to rally around, because the very mention of lack sends most people running (often to other anxiety-inducing activities that promise more). Rallying in this way would involve sustaining anxiety rather than obliterating it.[27] It would mean recognizing the D (singular and multiple) as a lost cause.

5
Libidinal Ecology

We have become used to a certain version of ecomelancholia. We are saturated by it. Our lost objects are endless. There are the vanishing forests, the starving polar bears, and the daily horrors of the meat industry. There is the rapid melting of the polar ice caps and ocean acidification, a staggering reduction in biodiversity, and insect die-off, not to mention the infinity of plastic buildup that is choking what's left. Even our clearest hope for a better future, renewable energy, comes at a cost.[1] Meanwhile, environmental racism continues apace in Black, Brown, and Indigenous communities, and oil companies like Exxon Mobil continue to rake in profits.[2]

It doesn't end there. Mega fires are becoming more frequent and far deadlier. COVID-19 has spread to all corners of the earth. To say that the virus kills is, of course, true; COVID-19 has devastated whole populations (again, mostly Black, Brown, and poor) the world over. But the greater truth is that nothing is more viral than this vampire economy we live by, which lives on our broken flesh.

Of course, these events are all tied to climate peril. The planet's devastation disrupts and dislocates complex ecosystems, increasing the likelihood that what seems catastrophic now will be an ordinary day in the not-so-distant future.

Between those who profit from disaster and those who suffer from it, there stands another major threat to life—the police. Anti-Black terrorism and the armies of militarized police are the first lines of defense in maintaining not our safety but private property, white supremacy, and bipartisan neoliberalism. Adding insult to injury, the police are organized. Their budgets are fat, in the order of several billions of dollars. Meanwhile, our schools, our commons, and our bodies rot from austerity.

Ecomelancholia isn't an aberrant condition; it is, rather, the general psychosomatic condition of being alive today and conscious of the growing destitution of the planet. Some of us (white, cisgender, affluent) may be able to pretend it isn't happening—for a while, anyway. But the global destitution is coming; the end of the world is already here. It's been here.[3]

Faced with this generalized loss, left-wing academics have turned to deconstructed particulars, endless mourning, and a politics of spectrality at the expense of universalist communist struggle. Although I am sympathetic to spectral politics and am not immune to the deconstructive argument, with Wendy Brown and Jodi Dean,[4] I am left to wonder how hauntology leads to emancipatory struggle. How do we collectivize loss? Because, indeed, each loss is singular and unequivocal, as leftist melancholy attests; but the *libidinal* connection to loss is universal. Loss, as Freud and Lacan both argue, drives eros.

A Planet to Lose

Leftist melancholy has hitherto only theorized the lost attachment; it has yet to theorize the object of destitution, which the psychoanalytic subject willingly abandons in order to *enjoy* a spacious (and specious) loss. We can imagine the consequence of focusing only on the first half of this loss. The result is a game show style of politics, in which everyone gets their own lost object: "You get a specter! And you get a specter!"[5] But if we are to imagine collective, emancipatory struggle, we will need to go beyond leftist melancholy, with its endless, atomized particulars. We'll need to theorize leftist eros.

Unlike leftist melancholy, which waxes on about an impossible transcendental object and so oddly enough continues to pay homage to the signifier of lost plentitude (Lacan calls this way of enjoyment phallic jouissance and attributes it to the masculine position in his theory of sexuation), leftist eros (which we could align with the feminine position, keeping in mind that these terms "feminine" and "masculine" are purely symbolic coordinates) accepts its castration and the destitution of the phallus as the true driving force of libidinal politics, *all* politics, right and left.[6]

The Right knows this. While the Left has been busy with hauntology, the Right has had a monopoly on libidinal politics, which reached its zenith (or nadir) in the Trump presidency. To be adherent to Trump and all that the Right symbolizes (including white supremacy, ecoapartheid, and capitalist annihilation) is to be libidinally cathected to the sacrificial, self-destructive politics of Trump's rhetoric. That enjoyment is not incidental to the inconsistencies in Trump's speech (his contradictions, falsities, and incoherence). Nor is it incidental to his sadism. While liberals point to the inconsistencies in Trump's speech, to his buffoonery and ineptitude, they miss the enjoyment that Trump inspires in his followers. Their enjoyment is directly wired to Trump's nonsense—to the lack he symbolizes and quite clearly enjoys.

Contrast Trump's rhetoric to the sterile discourse of liberals and most leftists, and we begin to see a problem. The problem was recently diagnosed in the fourth installment of *The Matrix* series, *Resurrections* (2021), when the Analyst scoffs at the importance of facts: "[The old] Matrix was all fussy facts and equations," the Analyst derides. "But [people] don't give a shit about facts," he says. "It's all about fiction."⁷ The Analyst is the film's figure of right-wing authority, but he makes a good point. The Left has had a monopoly on facts, but it has little to say about the fictions that trigger our enjoyment.

Consider an example. In their conclusion to *A Planet to Win: Why We Need a Green New Deal*, coauthors Kate Aronoff, Alyssa Battistoni, Daniel Cohen, and Thea Riofrancos invite readers to envision "a possible near-future." That future includes "workers around the country . . . planting trees in degraded forests," "intercity travel that's carbon-free," "tuition-free college," and "guaranteed jobs" that "pay a good wage for a four-day week."⁸ Key here is that the authors stress enjoyment. The future they hold out for is one in which we get to enjoy life without the barriers that capitalism imposes. They warn that the "carbon-free, communal luxuries that a radical Green New Deal promises" are not all "just around the corner." Nevertheless, they maintain, "we should keep these visions of a possible near-future in mind as we tackle the devilish details of decarbonizing."⁹ Aronoff and her cowriters argue that the fight for decarbonization should be "all-out"; there's no time to lose.¹⁰ This is especially true of a climate strike. In their outline of a Green New Deal, they "call for 100 percent all-out strike: shutting down business as usual to make a new order possible."¹¹ The problem, as I see it, is that this strategy for the future considers enjoyment as the endpoint, after the strike and after the obstacles have been surmounted. But this misses the enjoyment that the drive already obtains in the present through loss. As Todd McGowan argues, the problem isn't that capitalism blocks our enjoyment, erecting barriers where there would otherwise be free-flowing desire; the problem is that we enjoy the barriers.¹² The basic insight of psychoanalysis is this: we are not driven to sustain ourselves or the environment or multispecies beings. Sorry. We are, according to Freud, driven to repeat actions that jeopardize our well-being.

Aronoff and company are hyperaware of loss, so much so that their visions of loss nearly outnumber their visions of success: "There will be setbacks"; "The more serious a climate program we have, the more opposition it will face"; "Political change is uneven and multifaceted."[13] These caveats spread throughout *A Planet to Win* and, at least on the surface, signify the authors' pragmatism.

Nevertheless, the repetition of loss in their book suggests that there is more than mere pragmatism at stake in their rhetoric. Read psychoanalytically, the losses that interrupt their progressive narrative are, in fact, central, not peripheral, to the enjoyment they incur in writing and imagining climate activism. I am suggesting that Aronoff and her coauthors underestimate the value of loss both in their own writing and in motivating large-scale decarbonization. From this vantage, the rhetoric of left environmentalism should not be "a planet to win" but "a planet to lose." If we take the death drive seriously, as thinkers like Lee Edelman and Alenka Zupančič do, then an ecological politics based on winning can never truly succeed, since winning conceals the traumatic structure that brings people to the streets.

I am not suggesting that the future imagined by the authors of *A Planet to Win* is in any way naive. Nor am I arguing that we should not be concerned with practical matters, only the pure negativity of the drive. Death drive does not have to be an edgelord discourse.[14] Instead, I am trying to tap the creativity and superfluity of the drive for a truly "all-out" strike.

Consider a final example. In her COP26 speech, delivered to a mass rally of climate protestors, Greta Thunberg did her usual routine: she quoted the facts about carbon emissions, excoriated governmental officials, and urged her audience to listen to the scientists. Despite the usual rhetoric (listen to the scientists!), one intriguing speech act broke through. Thunberg said to her audience, "No more blah blah blah."[15] This speech act, which privileges the jouissance of the signifier, its sheer sonic repetition over meaning, was soon repeated, memed, and hashtagged and became part of the strike's verbal arsenal. At its core, however, "No more blah blah blah" is rhetorically powerful because it taps the nonsensical, meaningless, and afutural Real of the signifier that Lacan, in his reading of James Joyce, claims drives Joyce's literary inventiveness.[16] Not a mere negation of the future, then, the death drive motivates Joyce's creativity, forging new linguistic pathways and bonds that previously did not exist. This, to my mind, is a pretty good example of what left-wing politics can do: forge coalitions, creating surplus *from* lack. To be clear, I am not saying that Thunberg is the Joyce of the environmental Left. I am saying, however, that Thunberg, in her speech, unintentionally touched on the sacrificial energy of the drive, a drive that has no future and no fight to win but is crucial to going *all out*.

The Jouissance of Sacrifice

In one of the great anticapitalist films of the twentieth century, Frank Capra's *It's a Wonderful Life* (1946), we follow the life of George Bailey (James Stewart), a banker's son who has inherited (unwillingly) his father's business and, with it, the trauma of unfulfillment.[17] Bailey, we learn in flashback, has spent his life dreaming of escaping his small town, Bedford Falls, and becoming an adventurer, a world traveler, a man without limits. His dreams quickly disintegrate. He sacrifices his body as a young boy to save his younger brother from drowning in a freezing lake, losing his hearing in one ear as a result. Later, he sacrifices his body again to save his childhood employer, Mr. Gower (H. B. Warner), the pharmacist who has made a terrible, grief-stricken mistake mixing poison with medication, by not delivering the medicine and receiving several blows to his damaged ear from the drunken Gower for his trouble. Last but not least, he takes on the full symbolic weight of his castration by sacrificing his dream of traveling the world, attending college, and, later, his dream of the perfect honeymoon, saving his father's business from the mercenary greed of the town villain, Mr. Potter (Lionel Barrymore). When Bailey has finally lost everything, when his destitution is near complete because his business partner has misplaced eight thousand dollars, effectively bankrupting their business and the community, Bailey throws himself at the mercy of Potter, who, in good capitalist fashion, retorts that Bailey is worth more to his family and friends dead than alive. Internalizing this logic and haunted by the thought that his wife, Mary Bailey (Donna Reed), would have been happier with his friend and symbolic rival, Sam Wainwright (Frank Albertson), who has made a fortune in plastics, he abandons all he has left (wife, children, dilapidated home), unable to confront the obscene underside of his libidinal career—not his manifest life as a reluctant banker, husband, and father but his unconscious life of destitution. Though he feels bereft, robbed of everything he has worked for and dreamed of, the true, unspeakable core of his life is that it has been spent repeating the act of destitution over and over. Although sacrifice is the unconscious source of Bailey's enjoyment, he has yet to embrace destitution as a radical act.

This all changes when he begins to see that the world would be poorer without him and that his propensity to lose isn't a shortcoming but a boon. Though Bailey has been running from the castrating memory of his father's failures all his life, at the end of the movie, by dint of a miracle, he learns that his failures have been fecund. He is richer for losing.

Bailey chooses life. More importantly, he chooses a life of destitution. In the film's final scene, Bailey returns to his family as a man returned from the dead, joyful for all that has come from his sacrificial career. Were that all, the film would end with an insightful psychoanalytic lesson on the true nature of enjoyment. Unlike Mr. Potter, who seemingly has everything, Bailey is destitute (his business bankrupt, his home derelict, his children poorly dressed for want of money, his wife, named Mary no less, deprived of everything he feels she rightly deserves), but he lacks nothing in the company of those who share his lack. This, the film suggests, is the true definition of communism: sharing what we don't have. And yet the film builds on this psychoanalytic point about loss by taking what is, in essence, the work of each analysand (learning to enjoy one's lack) and putting it in the realm of collective politics. Bailey does not lose everything. His brother calls him "the richest man in town," because everyone sacrifices on his behalf: his brother, Mr. Gower, Sam, and so on. Everyone who has benefited from his life of destitution sacrifices to keep his libidinal career going.

Bailey does not die. His prayer, "I want to live, God, I want to live," is answered. *It's a Wonderful Life* embraces the bewildering, idiosyncratic truth of events—that is, miracles—and gives form to the miracle through the senseless repetition of the drive.[18] Miraculously, paradoxically, it is the death drive—the very form of nothing—that saves Bailey in the end (figure 16). In the film's final scene, we see all whom Bailey's senseless self-destruction has touched come together in righteous, libidinal celebration of the lack that binds them (figure 17). Down with Mr. Potter (symbol of capitalist nihilism)! Up with destitution (object-cause of leftist enjoyment)!

Can we, like Bailey and company, become a Left of the miracle and no longer a Left beholden to eco-utopianism (the environmental wager), hauntological defeatism (the academic wager), expertise (the technocratic wager), or cynical managerialism (the liberal democratic wager)? Can we, like Bailey, learn to enjoy loss?

Although I can't promise that enjoying loss will grant leftists their wings, I am betting on losing.

FIG. 16. Still from *It's a Wonderful Life* (1946).

FIG. 17. Still from *It's a Wonderful Life* (1946).

NOTES

PROVOCATIONS

1. Jean-Paul Sartre, *Being and Nothingness: An Essay on Phenomenological Ontology*, trans. Hazel E. Barnes (New York: Routledge, 2003), 45.
2. Jacques Lacan, *The Seminar of Jacques Lacan, Book II: The Ego in Freud's Theory and in the Technique of Psychoanalysis, 1954–1955*, trans. Sylvana Tomaselli (New York: Norton, 1988), 223.
3. Tiqqun, *Introduction to Civil War*, trans. Alexander R. Galloway and Jason E. Smith (Los Angeles: Semiotext(e), 2010), 145–46.

PREFACE

1. Donald J. Trump (@realDonaldTrump), "STOP THE COUNT!" X, November 5, 2020, 8:12 a.m., https://x.com/realDonaldTrump/status/1324353932022480896.
2. Aaron Rupar, "Trump's Desperate 'STOP THE COUNT!' Tweet, Briefly Explained," Vox, November 5, 2020, https://www.vox.com/2020/11/5/21550880/trump-tweet-stop-the-count-votes-presidential-election.
3. Igor Derysh, "Joe Biden to Rich Donors: 'Nothing Would Fundamentally Change' If He's Elected," Salon, June 19, 2019, https://www.salon.com/2019/06/19/joe-biden-to-rich-donors-nothing-would-fundamentally-change-if-hes-elected/.
4. On algorithmic power, see, for example, Cathy O'Neil, *Weapons of Math Destruction: How Big Data Increases Inequality and Threatens Democracy* (New York: Crown, 2016); Jackie Wang, *Carceral Capitalism* (South Pasadena CA: Semiotext(e), 2018), 42–56; and Ian Alan

Paul, "Anaesthetic Violence," *Ill Will*, December 15, 2023, https://illwill.com/anaesthetic-violence. Paul deploys the term "anaesthetic" as a corrective to Jacques Rancière's influential theory of aesthetic numbering. "Anaesthetic violence counts lives ever more exactly only so it can ever more precisely calculate their devastation."

5. Alain Badiou, *Being and Event*, trans. Oliver Feltham (London: Continuum, 2005), 23–25. Badiou defines the social order, or "situation," in his lexicon as countable. We *are* only insofar as we count within a given number or set. By contrast, the event qua inconsistent void suspends the situation, inducing subjects who become uncountable through fidelity to the event's impossible possibility.

6. Jacques Rancière, *Disagreement: Politics and Philosophy*, trans. Julie Rose (Minneapolis: University of Minnesota Press, 1999), 29–30.

7. See, for example, Saidiya V. Hartman, *Scenes of Subjection: Terror, Slavery, and Self-Making in Nineteenth-Century America* (New York: Oxford University Press, 1997); David Marriott, *Whither Fanon? Studies in the Blackness of Being* (Stanford CA: Stanford University Press, 2018); Calvin L. Warren, *Ontological Terror: Blackness, Nihilism, and Emancipation* (Durham NC: Duke University Press, 2018); Frank B. Wilderson III, *Red, White, and Black: Cinema and the Structure of U.S. Antagonisms* (Durham NC: Duke University Press, 2010); and Frank B. Wilderson III, *Afropessimism* (New York: Liveright, 2020).

8. On a concept related to destituent ecology, see Todd McGowan's theory of "nonbelonging" in *Enjoyment Right and Left* (Minneapolis: Sublation Press, 2022). "Leftism," McGowan writes, "or the emancipatory project is the embrace of the radical enjoyment of contradiction, the enjoyment of nonbelonging" (19).

9. Alain Badiou, *Conditions*, trans. Steven Corcoran (London: Continuum, 2008), 110.

10. E. M. Forster, *Howards End* (New York: Alfred A. Knopf, 1991), 195. For a sustained critique of ecocritical affirmation and the logics of connection that subtend it, see Steven Swarbrick and Jean-Thomas Tremblay, *Negative Life: The Cinema of Extinction* (Evanston IL: Northwestern University Press, 2024).

11. Gilles Deleuze and Félix Guattari, *A Thousand Plateaus: Capitalism and Schizophrenia*, trans. Brian Massumi (Minneapolis: University of Minnesota Press, 1987), 15.

12. Frédéric Neyrat, *Atopias: Manifesto for a Radical Existentialism*, trans. Walt Hunter and Lindsay Turner (New York: Fordham University Press, 2018), 4.
13. Jacques Lacan, *The Seminar of Jacques Lacan, Book XX: On Feminine Sexuality, the Limits of Love and Knowledge, 1972–1973*, ed. Jacques-Alain Miller, trans. Bruce Fink (New York: Norton, 1998), 57.
14. Lacan defines the uncountable as the impossible Real, the site of the partial object and drive. Badiou, who follows Lacan to a point, defines the uncountable as the empty set, the site of absence within a given structure or world.

1. OUTSIDE IN THE ECOLOGICAL MACHINE

1. See, for example, John Bellamy Foster, *Marx's Ecology: Materialism and Nature* (New York: Monthly Review Press, 2000); Andreas Malm, *Corona, Climate, Chronic Emergency: War Communism in the Twenty-First Century* (London: Verso, 2020); Søren Mau, *Mute Compulsion: A Marxist Theory of the Economic Power of Capital* (London: Verso, 2023); Kohei Saito, *Marx in the Anthropocene: Towards the Idea of Degrowth Communism* (Cambridge: Cambridge University Press, 2022); The Salvage Collective, *The Tragedy of the Worker: Towards the Proletarocene* (London: Verso, 2021); and Kate Soper, *Post-Growth Living: For an Alternative Hedonism* (London: Verso, 2023).
2. Quoted in H.D., *Tribute to Freud* (New York: New Directions, 2012), 18.
3. Nicole Seymour, *Bad Environmentalism: Irony and Irreverence in the Ecological Age* (Minneapolis: University of Minnesota Press, 2018).
4. Lacan compares the libido to a shape-shifting amoeba and nicknames it "lamella" in *The Seminar of Jacques Lacan, Book XI: The Four Fundamental Concepts of Psychoanalysis*, ed. Jacques-Alain Miller, trans. Alan Sheridan (New York: Norton, 1998), 197. Slavoj Žižek takes this amoeboid comparison to its horrifying conclusion in his discussion of the film *Alien* (1979): "The alien is libido as pure life, indestructible and immortal." Slavoj Žižek, *How to Read Lacan* (New York: Norton, 2006), 63.
5. Freud articulates this point: "The finding of an object is in fact a refinding of it," in *Three Essays on the Theory of Sexuality* (1905), in *The Standard Edition of the Complete Psychological Works of Sigmund*

Freud, vol. 7, ed. and trans. James Strachey (London: Hogarth Press and the Institute of Psychoanalysis, 1953–74), 222.

6. Jason W. Moore uses the term "web of life" to denote "the biological and geological conditions of capitalism's process" in *Capitalism in the Web of Life: Ecology and the Accumulation of Capital* (New York: Verso, 2015), 2–3.

7. Freudian metapsychology could thus be read as a highly combustible example of the aesthetics of petroleum, to use Stephanie LeMenager's term in *Living Oil: Petroleum Culture in the American Century* (Oxford: Oxford University Press, 2014). LeMenager references Freud briefly in her conceptualization of "petromelancholia" (105).

8. See, for example, Lawrence Buell, *Writing for an Endangered World: Literature, Culture, and Environment in the U.S. and Beyond* (Cambridge MA: Belknap Press of Harvard University Press, 2001), 22; and Mark Bould, *The Anthropocene Unconscious: Climate Catastrophe in Contemporary Culture* (London: Verso, 2021).

9. Moore, *Capitalism in the Web of Life*, 14.

10. Sigmund Freud, "Negation" (1925), in *The Standard Edition of the Complete Psychological Works of Sigmund Freud*, vol. 19, ed. and trans. James Strachey (London: Hogarth Press and the Institute of Psychoanalysis, 1953–74), 237.

11. Freud, "Negation," 237.

12. Frédéric Neyrat theorizes this lack of exit, in which life becomes claustrophobic, as "saturated immanence" in *Atopias: Manifesto for a Radical Existentialism*, trans. Walt Hunter and Lindsay Turner (New York: Fordham University Press, 2018), 4.

13. Jacques Lacan, *Anxiety: The Seminar of Jacques Lacan, Book X*, ed. Jacques-Alain Miller, trans. A. R. Price (Malden MA: Polity Press, 2016), 54.

14. Lacan, *Anxiety*, 327–28.

15. Karen Barad, *Meeting the Universe Halfway: Quantum Physics and the Entanglement of Matter and Meaning* (Durham NC: Duke University Press, 2007), 140.

16. I develop this point elsewhere. See Steven Swarbrick, *The Environmental Unconscious: Ecological Poetics from Spenser to Milton* (Minneapolis: University of Minnesota Press, 2023), 3, 9–17; and

Steven Swarbrick, "The Weather in Sedgwick," *Critical Inquiry* 49, no. 2 (2023): 165–84.

17. Lacan, *Four Fundamental Concepts of Psychoanalysis*, 23; emphasis in the original.
18. See Steven Swarbrick and Jean-Thomas Tremblay, *Negative Life: The Cinema of Extinction* (Evanston IL: Northwestern University Press, 2024), 7–8.
19. *Mad Men*, created by Matthew Weiner (Santa Monica CA: Lionsgate Television, Weiner Bros., American Movie Classics, UROK Productions, 2007–15).
20. Todd McGowan elucidates this point in *Capitalism and Desire: The Psychic Cost of Free Markets* (New York: Columbia University Press, 2016), see especially 36–41.
21. Frédéric Neyrat, *The Unconstructable Earth: An Ecology of Separation*, trans. Drew S. Burk (New York: Fordham University Press, 2019), 183.
22. Lacan uses the terms "alienation" and "separation" to explain, first, our symbolic capture and, second, our symbolic destitution. The advent of the subject only comes about, Lacan theorizes, by subtracting our place in the symbolic order. He calls this formal subtraction "destitution." For a lucid account of Lacan's conceptual pair, alienation and separation, see Paul Verhaeghe, "Lacan's Answer to Alienation: Separation," *Crisis and Critique* 6, no. 1 (2019): 365–88. The term "subjective destitution" appears throughout Žižek's writing. See, for example, Slavoj Žižek, *The Metastases of Enjoyment: On Women and Causality* (London: Verso, 2005), 167–72; and Slavoj Žižek, "The Minimal Event: From Hystericization to Subjective Destitution," in *Repeating Žižek*, ed. Agon Hamza (Durham NC: Duke University Press, 2015), 269–85.
23. Saidiya Hartman, "The End of White Supremacy, an American Romance," *Bomb* 152 (June 5, 2020), https://bombmagazine.org/articles/the-end-of-white-supremacy-an-american-romance/.
24. Hartman, "The End of White Supremacy."
25. "I am in death's position," says the speaker in Claudia Rankine's *Don't Let Me Be Lonely: An American Lyric* (Minneapolis MN: Graywolf Press, 2004), 7.
26. Kai Heron and Jodi Dean, "Revolution or Ruin," *e-flux* 110 (June

2020), https://www.e-flux.com/journal/110/335242/revolution-or-ruin/.
27. Anna Kornbluh, "Extinct Critique," *South Atlantic Quarterly* 119, no. 4 (2020): 770–71.
28. Kornbluh, "Extinct Critique," 772.
29. Gilles Deleuze and Félix Guattari, *A Thousand Plateaus: Capitalism and Schizophrenia*, trans. Brian Massumi (Minneapolis: University of Minnesota Press, 1987), 130.
30. Ecocriticism's embrace of deconstruction begins with this Derridean intervention, which supports the idea that nature is a fluid, differential tapestry or a congealed performativity, not a fixed thing. See, for example, Matthias Fritsch, Philippe Lynes, and David Wood, eds., *Eco-Deconstruction: Derrida and Environmental Philosophy* (New York: Fordham University Press, 2018).
31. See Jacques Derrida, *Speech and Phenomena and Other Essays on Husserl's Theory of Signs*, trans. David B. Allison (Evanston IL: Northwestern University Press, 1973). Derrida's critique of Husserlian phenomenology begins with a devastating insight: "Phenomenology seems to us tormented, if not contested from within, by its own descriptions of the movement of temporalization and of the constitution of intersubjectivity. At the heart of what ties together these two decisive moments of description we recognize an irreducible nonpresence as having a constituting value, and with it a nonlife, a nonpresence or nonself-belonging of the living present, an ineradicable nonprimordiality" (6–7). Husserl and the phenomenological tradition after him presuppose a primordial "living present" beneath and beyond metaphysical abstraction. This "living present"—this tormenting fiction—grounds phenomenology and, Derrida contends, ungrounds it *at the same time* (time, of course, being the issue, because time, for Derrida, is nonidentical and nonpresent).
32. Derrida, *Speech and Phenomena*, 128.
33. "Enlightenment is totalitarian," Horkheimer and Adorno write. See Max Horkheimer and Theodor W. Adorno, *Dialectic of Enlightenment: Philosophical Fragments*, trans. Edmund Jephcott (Stanford CA: Stanford University Press, 2002), 4.
34. The term "flat ontology" derives from Manuel DeLanda's *Intensive Science and Virtual Philosophy* (London: Bloomsbury, 2002), 51.

Fellow proponents of flat ontology or variants of it include Bruno Latour, Graham Harman (and object-oriented ontology, or OOO), Ian Bogost, and Jane Bennett.

35. Todd McGowan, "Objects after Subjects: Hegel's Broken Ontology," in *Subject Lessons: Hegel, Lacan, and the Future of Materialism*, ed. Russell Sbriglia and Slavoj Žižek (Evanston IL: Northwestern University Press, 2020), 68–81.

36. G. W. F. Hegel, *Phenomenology of Spirit*, trans. A. V. Miller (Oxford: Oxford University Press, 1977), 10.

37. *Titane*, directed by Julia Ducournau (Paris: Kazak Productions, Frakas Productions, Arte France Cinéma, VOO, BeTV, 2021).

38. Martin Heidegger, "The Origin of the Work of Art," in *Poetry, Language, Thought*, trans. Albert Hofstadter (New York: Harper Perennial, 1971), 32–36.

39. On this point, see Eugenie Brinkema, *Life-Destroying Diagrams* (Durham NC: Duke University Press, 2022): "Violence is not absorbed and brought to a close by sensitivity to the mutual relations of objects, but rather is spectacularly *increased*" (130).

40. See Jacques Lacan, *. . . or Worse: The Seminar of Jacques Lacan, Book XIX*, ed. Jacques-Alain Miller, trans. A. R. Price (Medford MA: Polity Press, 2018), 88–94.

41. William Shakespeare, *As You Like It*, in *The Norton Shakespeare*, 3rd ed., ed. Stephen Greenblatt et al. (New York: Norton, 2016), act 2, scene 1, lines 16–17.

42. *Twin Peaks: The Return*, part 14, directed by David Lynch (New York: Showtime Networks, Rancho Rosa Partnership, Twin Peaks Productions, Lynch/Frost Productions, 2017).

43. See, for example, Jacqueline Rose's classic *Sexuality in the Field of Vision* (1986; repr., London: Verso, 2005); and Joan Copjec, *Read My Desire: Lacan against the Historicists* (1994; repr., London: Verso, 2015).

2. THE EARTH IS EVIL

1. *Melancholia*, directed by Lars von Trier (Hvidovre, Denmark: Zentropa Entertainments, Memfis Film, Zentropa International Sweden, Slot Machine, Liberator Productions, Zentropa International Köln, Film i Väst, Danmarks Radio, Arte France Cinéma, 2011).

2. Quoted in Manohla Dargis, "This Is How the End Begins," *New York Times*, December 30, 2011, http://www.nytimes.com/2012/01/01/movies/awardsseason/manohla-dargis-looks-at-the-overture-to-melancholia.html.
3. Dargis, "This Is How the End Begins."
4. This, for example, is Timothy Morton's argument in *Hyperobjects: Philosophy and Ecology after the End of the World* (Minneapolis: University of Minnesota Press, 2013): "As I shall argue, the strongly held belief that the world is about to end 'unless we act now' is paradoxically one of the most powerful factors that inhibit a full engagement with our ecological coexistence here on Earth. . . . The end of the world has already occurred" (6–7).
5. On this point, see Steven Shaviro, "MELANCHOLIA or, the Romantic Anti-Sublime," *Sequence* 1, no. 1 (2012): 6–9, https://reframe.sussex.ac.uk/sequence1/1-1-melancholia-or-the-romantic-anti-sublime/.
6. Cultural studies of melodrama have criticized the genre for masking issues of structural inequality under signs of personal and domestic strife. See, for example, Lauren Berlant, *The Female Complaint: The Unfinished Business of Sentimentality in American Culture* (Durham NC: Duke University Press, 2008); and Elizabeth R. Anker, *Orgies of Feeling: Melodrama and the Politics of Freedom* (Durham NC: Duke University Press, 2014). Jonathan Goldberg, *Melodrama: An Aesthetics of Impossibility* (Durham NC: Duke University Press, 2016), ix.
7. Alain Badiou, "On Evil: An Interview with Alain Badiou," interview by Christoph Cox and Molly Whalen, *Cabinet* 5 (Winter 2001), http://www.cabinetmagazine.org/issues/5/cox_whalen_badiou.php.
8. Badiou, "On Evil."
9. Badiou, "On Evil."
10. Badiou, "On Evil."
11. Badiou, "On Evil."
12. Bonnie Honig connects John's catastrophe denialism to the rhetoric of "fake news" espoused by the Trump administration and Far Right. "Invoking his own preferred scientists," Honig writes, "John forecasts a near miss." See Bonnie Honig, "No Collision," *Boston Review*, December 8, 2018, http://bostonreview.net/science-nature-politics/bonnie-honig-no-collision.

13. Joan Copjec, *Imagine There's No Woman: Ethics and Sublimation* (Cambridge MA: MIT Press, 2002), 34–37.
14. D. W. Winnicott, "Transitional Objects and Transitional Phenomena: A Study of the First Not-Me Possession," *International Journal of Psychoanalysis* 34 (1953): 89–97.
15. Bonnie Honig, "'Out Like a Lion': *Melancholia* with Euripides and Winnicott," *Theory and Event* 18, no. 2 (2015), https://muse.jhu.edu/article/578625.
16. William E. Connolly, *The Fragility of Things: Self-Organizing Processes, Neoliberal Fantasies, and Democratic Activism* (Durham NC: Duke University Press, 2013), 47.
17. Jacques Lacan, *The Seminar of Jacques Lacan, Book XI: The Four Fundamental Concepts of Psychoanalysis*, ed. Jacques-Alain Miller, trans. Alan Sheridan (New York: Norton, 1998), 25.
18. Jacques Lacan, *The Seminar of Jacques Lacan, Book XX: On Feminine Sexuality, the Limits of Love and Knowledge, 1972–1973*, ed. Jacques-Alain Miller, trans. Bruce Fink (New York: Norton, 1998), 7. Alain Badiou offers a close approximation of the ecological unconscious I posit via Freud. His mathematical ontology strictly in-consists: there is structure, there is the order of the count, and there is void. Badiou will occasionally call the void *das Ding*, after Lacan. Badiou's ontology is, therefore, a radical attempt to extend psychoanalysis into the order of being. See Alain Badiou, *Second Manifesto for Philosophy*, trans. Louise Burchill (Malden MA: Polity Press, 2011). For a related theory of ontological lack, see Mari Ruti's late essay, "The Brokenness of Being," *Angelaki* 28, no. 6 (2023): 123–70, which considers lack (dislocation, dispossession) not just a human condition but a condition of being as such.
19. On the "unconstructability" of the earth and its consequences for environmental thought, see Frédéric Neyrat, *The Unconstructable Earth: An Ecology of Separation*, trans. Drew S. Burk (New York: Fordham University Press, 2019).
20. I derive the term "autological subject" from Elizabeth A. Povinelli's *The Empire of Love: Toward a Theory of Intimacy, Genealogy, and Carnality* (Durham NC: Duke University Press, 2006), 4.
21. On "thought without image," see Gilles Deleuze, *Difference and Repetition*, trans. Paul Patton (New York: Columbia University

Press, 1994), 147. For a related theory of politics as disimaging, see Alain Badiou, *Images of the Present Time*, trans. Susan Spitzer (New York: Columbia University Press, 2023).

22. Alenka Zupančič, *What Is Sex?* (Cambridge MA: MIT Press, 2017), 104.

23. Thomas Elsaesser, "Tales of Sound and Fury: Observations on the Family Melodrama," in *Imitations of Life: A Reader on Film and Television Melodrama*, ed. Marcia Landy (Detroit MI: Wayne State University Press, 1991), 74.

24. Jonathan Goldberg, "Fidelio: Melodramas of Agency and Identity," *Criticism* 55, no. 4 (2013): 554.

25. Fred Moten, *In the Break: The Aesthetics of the Black Radical Tradition* (Minneapolis: University of Minnesota Press, 2003).

26. Andrea Long Chu, *Females* (London: Verso, 2019), 22.

27. Frank B. Wilderson III, *Afropessimism* (New York: Liveright, 2020), 16–17.

28. Chu, *Females*, 11.

29. Jason W. Moore, *Capitalism in the Web of Life: Ecology and the Accumulation of Capital* (New York: Verso, 2015), 3.

30. Moore, *Capitalism in the Web of Life*, 8.

31. For a related critique of Moore's monism, see Kohei Saito, *Marx in the Anthropocene: Towards the Idea of Degrowth Communism* (Cambridge: Cambridge University Press, 2022), 114–31.

32. Lacan, *Seminar of Jacques Lacan, Book XX*, 59.

33. Claire Colebrook challenges postapocalyptic cinema's preservation of "the world," a world built on foundations of colonialism and anti-Blackness, asking whether such a world is ultimately worth saving. See Claire Colebrook, *Who Would You Kill to Save the World?* (Lincoln: University of Nebraska Press, 2023).

34. *Stars at Noon*, directed by Claire Denis (Paris: Curiosa Films, Arte France Cinéma, Ad Vitam Production, Canal+, ARTE, 2022).

35. Alain Badiou, *Theory of the Subject*, trans. Bruno Bosteels (London: Bloomsbury, 2009), 10–11.

36. Badiou, "On Evil."

37. On the neighbor as *das Ding*, object of radical unknowability and ethical object par excellence, see Kenneth Reinhard's "Toward a Political Theology of the Neighbor" and Slavoj Žižek's "Neighbors

and Other Monsters: A Plea for Ethical Violence," in *The Neighbor: Three Inquiries in Political Theology*, with Eric L. Santner (Chicago: University of Chicago Press, 2005), 11–75, 134–90.
38. Sigmund Freud, "Mourning and Melancholia" (1917), in *The Standard Edition of the Complete Psychological Works of Sigmund Freud*, vol. 14, ed. and trans. James Strachey (London: Hogarth Press and the Institute of Psychoanalysis, 1953–74), 245.
39. Frank B. Wilderson III, "'We're Trying to Destroy the World': Anti-Blackness and Police Violence after Ferguson," *Ill Will*, November 23, 2014, https://illwill.com/were-trying-to-destroy-the-world-anti-blackness-and-police-violence-after-ferguson.
40. As Saidiya Hartman writes in *Lose Your Mother: A Journey along the Atlantic Slave Route* (New York: Farrar, Straus, and Giroux, 2007), "The gaps and silences of my family were not unusual: slavery had made the past a mystery, unknowable and unspeakable" (13–14). Hartman's approach to the archive of Atlantic slavery could be described as the explication of those "gaps," a way of making a place for "silences" in the records of white supremacy.
41. Todd McGowan, *Enjoying What We Don't Have: The Political Project of Psychoanalysis* (Lincoln: University of Nebraska Press, 2013), 2.
42. McGowan, *Enjoying What We Don't Have*, 14.
43. See, for example, Mari Ruti, *The Singularity of Being: Lacan and the Immortal Within* (New York: Fordham University Press, 2012); and Mari Ruti, *The Ethics of Opting Out: Queer Theory's Defiant Subjects* (New York: Columbia University Press, 2017).
44. *2001: A Space Odyssey*, directed by Stanley Kubrick (London: Stanley Kubrick Productions, Metro-Goldwyn-Mayer, 1968).
45. On the two axes of the drive, see Adrian Johnston, *Time Driven: Metapsychology and the Splitting of the Drive* (Evanston IL: Northwestern University Press, 2005), xxxi–xxxii.
46. Jacques Lacan, "Position of the Unconscious," in *Écrits: The First Complete Edition in English*, trans. Bruce Fink (New York: Norton, 2006), 719.
47. The Heideggerian obsession with worldlessness is a constant of postwar continental philosophy and film, Roland Végső argues in *Worldlessness after Heidegger: Phenomenology, Psychoanalysis, Deconstruction* (Edinburgh: Edinburgh University Press, 2020). "In spite

of the fact that worldlessness designates the epochal catastrophe of our times, faced with the threat of the loss of the world, our philosophers have proceeded to produce ever more mesmerizing figures for this worldlessness." "Philosophy," especially post-Heideggerian philosophy, "incessantly promises to save us from the very thing it is assiduously preparing for us. It is in this sense that we could consider worldlessness to be something like a limit-concept of our historical moment" (4–5).

48. Zupančič, *What Is Sex?*, 138.
49. See Peter Szendy, *Apocalypse-Cinema: 2012 and Other Ends of the World*, trans. Will Bishop (New York: Fordham University Press, 2015), 1–4.

3. ZERO-WASTE SEX

1. Greta Thunberg (@GretaThunberg), "When you compare the overall current best available science to their insufficient, hypothetical 'climate targets' you clearly see that there's a gap, there are decades missing," Twitter, April 22, 2021, 1:42 p.m., https://twitter.com/GretaThunberg/status/1385303013376598020.
2. Thunberg, "When you compare."
3. Thunberg, "When you compare."
4. Adam Aton, "Biden Tells Congress Climate Action and Job Creation Are the Same," *Scientific American*, April 29, 2021, https://www.scientificamerican.com/article/biden-tells-congress-climate-action-and-job-creation-are-the-same/.
5. Daniel Strauss, "'Crisis into Opportunity': Biden Lays Out Vision for Sweeping Change in Speech to Congress," *Guardian*, April 28, 2021, https://www.theguardian.com/us-news/2021/apr/28/america-is-on-the-move-again-biden-to-give-first-congressional-address.
6. Thunberg, "When you compare."
7. On the pervasiveness of petrofictions in American culture, see Stephanie LeMenager, *Living Oil: Petroleum Culture in the American Century* (Oxford: Oxford University Press, 2014).
8. Timothy Morton defines "hyperobject" as an entity massively distributed in time and space in *Hyperobjects: Philosophy and Ecology after the End of the World* (Minneapolis: University of Minnesota Press, 2013).

9. Todd McGowan offers a lucid explanation of Lacan's objectified gaze in *The Real Gaze: Film Theory after Lacan* (Albany: State University of New York Press, 2007), 5–6.
10. Jennifer Friedlander, *Real Deceptions: The Contemporary Reinvention of Realism* (New York: Oxford University Press, 2017), 5.
11. Jane Bennett, *Vibrant Matter: A Political Ecology of Things* (Durham NC: Duke University Press, 2010).
12. Marx writes, "The philosophers have only *interpreted* the world, in various ways; the point, however, is to *change* it." Karl Marx, *Theses on Feuerbach*, in *The Marx-Engels Reader*, 2nd ed., ed. Robert C. Tucker (New York: Norton, 1978), 145. For comparison, see Gilles Deleuze's objection in *Cinema 2* regarding the "real" aim of Italian neorealism: "Is it not rather at the level of the 'mental,' in terms of thought? If all the movement-images, perceptions, actions and affects underwent such an upheaval, was this not first of all because a new element burst onto the scene which was to prevent perception being extended into action in order to put it in contact with thought." Gilles Deleuze, *Cinema 2: The Time-Image*, trans. Hugh Tomlinson and Robert Galeta (Minneapolis: University of Minnesota Press, 1989), 1. Deleuze reverses Marx's critique.
13. Here I draw on Claire Colebrook's claim that "thought possesses annihilating power" in *Sex after Life: Essays on Extinction, Vol. 2* (Ann Arbor MI: Open Humanities Press, 2014), 27; as well as Jean-Thomas Tremblay's sharp critique of ecological correctives in "Homeostasis and Extinction: Ted Chiang's 'Exhalation,'" *SubStance* 52, no. 1 (2023): 22–29. According to Tremblay, "Concepts like the Capitalocene and the Plantationocene enable us, as we contemplate the problem of futurelessness, to know the past and the present differently. Yet, because they are positioned as correctives to the Anthropocene, these terms, in the name of subverting a monolithic and universal human subject, retain it as a referent" (27). Tremblay argues against such correctives, asserting, in light of dire extinction, "thought can no longer look like itself" (27).
14. Kate Aronoff, *Overheated: How Capitalism Broke the Planet—And How We Fight Back* (New York: Bold Type Books, 2021), 345.
15. Cara New Daggett, *The Birth of Energy: Fossil Fuels, Thermodynamics,*

    Energy, and the Politics of Work (Durham NC: Duke University Press, 2019), 189.
16. Daggett, *Birth of Energy*, 193–94, 193.
17. Daggett, *Birth of Energy*, 186.
18. Daggett, *Birth of Energy*, 195.
19. Leo Bersani, "Is the Rectum a Grave?" in *Is the Rectum a Grave? And Other Essays* (Chicago: University of Chicago Press, 2010), 22.
20. Joan Copjec, *Read My Desire: Lacan against the Historicists* (1994; repr., London: Verso, 2015), 204.
21. Copjec, *Read My Desire*, 204.
22. I derive the term "subject supposed to know" from Jacques Lacan's *The Seminar of Jacques Lacan, Book XI: The Four Fundamental Concepts of Psychoanalysis*, ed. Jacques-Alain Miller, trans. Alan Sheridan (New York: Norton, 1998), 232. The subject supposed to know is the imaginary subject par excellence, embodied by the analyst and other figures of authority (God, teacher, scientist, police) and believed to have special access to truth. The subject supposed to know occupies the position of mastery in the analysand's unconscious fantasy, because they appear to have escaped symbolic castration, unlike everyone else. Ecocriticism is imaginary in precisely this way; it imagines a posthuman, interconnected, energy efficient, scientific, and sex-positive "subject supposed to know" who is undivided and who knows how to live rightly with nature and others.
23. This is Slavoj Žižek's argument in *The Sublime Object of Ideology* (London: Verso, 2008).
24. Mark Rifkin makes a related point in *Fictions of Land and Flesh* (Durham NC: Duke University Press, 2019): "The assumption of a shared set of terms, analyses, or horizons of political imagination between Black and Indigenous struggles may be premature or may obfuscate significant distinctions" (3). Rifkin foregrounds "Black and Indigenous political formations as something of a speculative leap" instead, involving "disoriented ... encounter with the other," rather than straightforward identification with a subject supposed to know (7).
25. Jacques Derrida's famous statement "there is no outside-text; *il n'y a pas de hors-texte*" is the implicit backdrop of ecodeconstruction, which posits nature as an endless, interwoven text. See Jacques

Derrida, *Of Grammatology*, trans. Gayatri Chakravorty Spivak (Chicago: University of Chicago Press, 1974), 158.

26. Stacy Alaimo theorizes the "transcorporeal" subject in *Exposed: Environmental Politics and Pleasures in Posthuman Times* (Minneapolis: University of Minnesota Press, 2016).

27. Here, I bend Lee Edelman's language of the futural fantasy toward an unlikely target: ecology. See Lee Edelman, *No Future: Queer Theory and the Death Drive* (Durham NC: Duke University Press, 2004). For a death-driven ecocriticism inspired by Edelman's queer negativity, see Steven Swarbrick, "Nature's Queer Negativity: Between Barad and Deleuze," *Postmodern Culture* 29, no. 2 (2019), https://doi.org/10.1353/pmc.2019.0003; and Steven Swarbrick, *Environmental Unconscious: Ecological Poetics from Spenser to Milton* (Minneapolis: University of Minnesota Press, 2023).

28. Ashley Dawson, *People's Power: Reclaiming the Energy Commons* (New York: OR Books, 2020), 3.

29. Sigmund Freud, *Three Essays on the Theory of Sexuality* (1905), in *The Standard Edition of the Complete Psychological Works of Sigmund Freud*, vol. 7, ed. and trans. James Strachey (London: Hogarth Press and the Institute of Psychoanalysis, 1953–74), 186–87.

30. Lacan, *Four Fundamental Concepts of Psychoanalysis*, 198.

31. See Frédéric Neyrat, *The Unconstructable Earth: An Ecology of Separation*, trans. Drew S. Burk (New York: Fordham University Press, 2019), 183.

32. Sigmund Freud, "Negation" (1925), in *The Standard Edition of the Complete Psychological Works of Sigmund Freud*, vol. 19, ed. and trans. James Strachey (London: Hogarth Press and the Institute of Psychoanalysis, 1953–74), 235.

33. Freud, "Negation," 235.

34. Freud, "Negation," 235.

35. Freud, "Negation," 235.

36. Freud, "Negation," 237–38.

37. Jacques Rancière, *The Politics of Aesthetics*, trans. Gabriel Rockhill (London: Continuum, 2004), 12–13.

38. Brian Massumi, *Parables for the Virtual: Movement, Affect, Sensation* (Durham NC: Duke University Press, 2002), 41.

39. Massumi, *Parables for the Virtual*, 42.

40. Massumi, *Parables for the Virtual*.
41. Dominic Boyer, *Energopolitics: Wind and Power in the Anthropocene* (Durham NC: Duke University Press, 2019).
42. Jonathan Crary, *24/7: Late Capitalism and the Ends of Sleep* (London: Verso, 2014).
43. See Mark Rifkin, *Beyond Settler Time: Temporal Sovereignty and Indigenous Self-Determination* (Durham NC: Duke University Press, 2017); Nick Estes, *Our History Is the Future: Standing Rock versus the Dakota Access Pipeline, and the Long Tradition of Indigenous Resistance* (London: Verso, 2019); and Macarena Gómez-Barris, *The Extractive Zone: Social Ecologies and Decolonial Perspectives* (Durham NC: Duke University Press, 2017).
44. See, for example, Imre Szeman and Dominic Boyer, eds., *Energy Humanities: An Anthology* (Baltimore MD: Johns Hopkins University Press, 2017). Despite its broad scope, the volume contains no sustained focus on the energopolitics of sex.
45. One exception is Michael Marder's *Energy Dreams: Of Actuality* (New York: Columbia University Press, 2017). See especially chapter 4, "Psychological Reveries."
46. *Night Moves*, directed by Kelly Reichardt (Los Angeles CA: Maybach Film Productions, RT Features, Film Science, DeLeon Productions, Tipping Point Productions, 2013).
47. Steven Hawley narrates the history of dam removal in America, from early ecoterrorist acts to mainstream environmentalism, in *Recovering a Lost River: Removing Dams, Rewilding Salmon, Revitalizing Communities* (Boston: Beacon Press, 2011), 5–11.
48. See Keith Makoto Woodhouse, *The Ecocentrists: A History of Radical Environmentalism* (New York: Columbia University Press, 2018).
49. On environmentalism's ecocidal contradictions, see Steven Swarbrick and Jean-Thomas Tremblay, *Negative Life: The Cinema of Extinction* (Evanston IL: Northwestern University Press, 2024), 127–51.
50. Katherine Fusco and Nicole Seymour, *Kelly Reichardt* (Urbana: University of Illinois Press, 2017), 3–4.
51. *12 Monkeys*, directed by Terry Gilliam (Los Angeles CA: Universal Pictures, Atlas Entertainment, Classico, Twelve Monkeys Productions, 1995); *Avengers: Endgame*, directed by Anthony Russo and Joe

Russo (Burbank CA: Marvel Studios, Walt Disney Pictures, 2019); *Tenet*, directed by Christopher Nolan (Burbank CA: Warner Bros., Syncopy, 2020).

52. Gómez-Barris, *Extractive Zone*, 96.
53. Gómez-Barris, *Extractive Zone*, 93, 97.
54. Antoine Traisnel, *Capture: American Pursuits and the Making of a New Animal Condition* (Minneapolis: University of Minnesota Press, 2020), 2.
55. Jackie Wang, *Carceral Capitalism* (South Pasadena CA: Semiotext(e), 2018), 40.
56. Walter Benjamin, "Theses on the Philosophy of History," in *Illuminations: Essays and Reflections*, ed. Hannah Arendt (New York: Schocken Books, 1969), 257.
57. Rifkin, *Beyond Settler Time*.
58. Fusco and Seymour, *Kelly Reichardt*, 81.
59. See James Martel, *The Misinterpellated Subject* (Durham NC: Duke University Press, 2017). On *aphanisis*, or the disappearance of the subject through alienation, see Lacan, *Four Fundamental Concepts of Psychoanalysis*, 218–19.
60. On the acausality of environmental action, see Jean-Thomas Tremblay, "Just Sabotage," *Critical Inquiry* 51, no. 1 (2024): 90–113. "The imperiling of narrative causality . . . reflects sabotage's crisis of sense[,] throw[ing] the semiotics of climate action into disarray" (107).

4. THE LOST D

1. Mari Ruti, *Penis Envy and Other Bad Feelings: The Emotional Costs of Everyday Life* (New York: Columbia University Press, 2018), 167.
2. Andreas Malm highlights the excessive enjoyment elicited by the SUV and pinpoints the connection between gas-guzzling automobiles and castration anxiety in *How to Blow Up a Pipeline* (London: Verso, 2021): "Never far below the surface, the terror of symbolic castration for owners who had invested not only class but manhood in their monster cars" (83).
3. This argument runs throughout McGowan's many books. See especially Todd McGowan, *Enjoying What We Don't Have: The Political Project of Psychoanalysis* (Lincoln: University of Nebraska Press,

2013); and Todd McGowan, *Capitalism and Desire: The Psychic Cost of Free Markets* (New York: Columbia University Press, 2016).
4. For trenchant accounts of anxiety and enjoyment from a Lacanian perspective, see, for example, Joan Copjec, *Read My Desire: Lacan against the Historicists* (1994; repr., London: Verso, 2015); and Slavoj Žižek, *Enjoy Your Symptom! Jacques Lacan in Hollywood and Out* (New York: Routledge, 2008).
5. *The Lost City*, directed by Aaron Nee and Adam Nee (West Hollywood CA: Paramount Pictures, 3dot Productions, Exhibit A, Fortis Films, 2022).
6. Jacques Lacan, *The Seminar of Jacques Lacan, Book XI: The Four Fundamental Concepts of Psychoanalysis*, ed. Jacques-Alain Miller, trans. Alan Sheridan (New York: Norton, 1998), 29.
7. *Yellowstone*, created by John Linson and Taylor Sheridan (Los Angeles CA: Paramount Network, 101 Studios, Linson Entertainment, Bosque Ranch Productions, Treehouse Films, MTV Entertainment Studios, 2018–24).
8. *Yellowstone*, season 3, episode 1, "You're the Indian Now," directed by Stephen Kay, written by Taylor Sheridan and John Linson, aired June 1, 2020, on Paramount Network.
9. See McGowan, *Capitalism and Desire*: "The capitalist system requires that subjects invest themselves in the idea of accumulation and the promise of an ultimate satisfaction that accompanies the idea. There is no capitalist subject—and thus no capitalist system—without that idea" (21).
10. For critical accounts of the multiple in radical theory, see Joan Copjec, "The Sexual Compact," *Angelaki* 17, no. 2 (2012): 31–48; Joan Copjec, "Sexual Difference," *Political Concepts: A Critical Lexicon*, November 3, 2014, https://www.politicalconcepts.org/sexual-difference-joan-copjec; and Ryan Engley and Todd McGowan, "Dualism and Multiplicity," *Why Theory*, podcast, March 19, 2022, 1:15, https://podcasts.apple.com/us/podcast/dualism-multiplicity/id1299863834?i=1000554586090.
11. *Toy Story*, directed by John Lasseter (Burbank CA: Walt Disney Pictures; Pixar Animation Studios, 1995).
12. See Alain Badiou, *Being and Event*, trans. Oliver Feltham (London: Continuum, 2005).

13. Patricia Heaton (@PatriciaHeaton), "Saw the trailer for Buzz Light-year and all I can say is Disney/Pixar made a HUGE mistake," Twitter, June 14, 2022, 10:48 a.m., https://twitter.com/PatriciaHeaton/status/1536737444804034561.
14. McGowan, *Enjoying What We Don't Have*, 16.
15. Brinkema's Heideggerian pronouncement that form has been forgotten is not a call to remember affect but an anxious call to remember the nothing (delay, trace, spacing, death) that informs formal analysis.
16. Brinkema states, "Neck is a trap. Luring with promises of theoretical reach, it shows in the end only the faint traces of a small patch of stirred skin, and it offers nothing new in the way of thought about texts themselves. Neck is antithetical to speculation. Decide—as in *decaedere*, cut off, cleave—to be done with one's own dull column." Eugenie Brinkema, *Life-Destroying Diagrams* (Durham NC: Duke University Press, 2022), 14.
17. Brinkema, *Life-Destroying Diagrams*, 6. Although the upshot of radical formalism is that it gives more, always more, and proffers the new (this is the Deleuzian thread running throughout Brinkema's book), we must consider the antinomy of this unrelenting "new" (20–21, 281). It is redundant. And because Brinkema opposes the new to the commodity form (5), we must ask also: Isn't the new precisely the spirit of capitalism and the commodity? The capitalist machine demands the new and is, to its credit, a radical formalist monster. Confronted with this zombielike insistence on the new, a more radical protest might be demanding the old, bad thing and familiar repetition, insisting that this new kills.
18. Martin Heidegger, *Being and Time*, trans. John Macquarrie and Edward Robinson (New York: Harper and Row, 1962), 21.
19. G. W. F. Hegel, *Phenomenology of Spirit*, trans. A. V. Miller (Oxford: Oxford University Press, 1977), 208; emphasis in the original.
20. See Lacan's formulas of sexuation in *The Seminar of Jacques Lacan, Book XX: On Feminine Sexuality, the Limits of Love and Knowledge, 1972–1973*, ed. Jacques-Alain Miller, trans. Bruce Fink (New York: Norton, 1998), 78.
21. As Copjec observes in "Sexual Difference," "Lacan once proffered the term 'being-towards-sex,' clearly referencing Heidegger's term

'being-towards-death,' in order presumably to displace the latter. The coinage of the new term goes beyond a simple terminological substitution by seeming to call for a rethinking of the arguments that led up to the original term. Whereas Heidegger links anxiety to the encounter with death, for example, Lacan insists that we see anxiety as, instead, an encounter with jouissance."

22. "Situations," Badiou writes in *Being and Event*, "are nothing more, in their being, than pure indifferent multiplicities.... The structure of situations does not, in itself, deliver any truths" (xii).

23. *Everything Everywhere All at Once*, directed by Daniel Kwan and Daniel Scheinert (New York: A24, IAC Films, AGBO, Year of the Rat, Ley Line Entertainment, 2022).

24. Todd McGowan, *Only a Joke Can Save Us: A Theory of Comedy* (Evanston IL: Northwestern University Press, 2017), 20–21.

25. See, for example, Kate Aronoff's conclusion to *Overheated: How Capitalism Broke the Planet—And How We Fight Back* (New York: Bold Type Books, 2021), where she posits the many benefits of ecosocialism. In *The Future Is Degrowth: A Guide to a World beyond Capitalism* (London: Verso, 2022), coauthors and degrowth advocates Matthias Schmelzer, Aaron Vansintjan, and Andrea Vetter critique the Green New Deal for mirroring the language of green capitalism with its promise of more. These authors rightly contend that we must content ourselves with *less* to avoid the worst climate scenarios. The degrowth movement calls for less accumulation; however, it does not make lack part of its political program. Degrowth champions limitation but fails to see limitation or lack as constitutive of the subject's libidinal makeup. By contrast, psychoanalysis maintains that abundance, whether capitalist or ecosocialist, is antithetical to desire since desire, per Lacan, desires what is absent.

26. See Lee Edelman, *No Future: Queer Theory and the Death Drive* (Durham NC: Duke University Press, 2004).

27. McGowan states, "One might embrace anxiety as an ethical and political choice." McGowan, *Enjoying What We Don't Have*, 112.

5. LIBIDINAL ECOLOGY

1. Jasper Bernes, "Between the Devil and the Green New Deal," *Commune*, April 25, 2019, https://communemag.com/between-the-devil

-and-the-green-new-deal/; Christopher Ketcham, "Addressing Climate Change Will Not 'Save the Planet,'" The Intercept, December 3, 2022, https://theintercept.com/2022/12/03/climate-biodiversity-green-energy/.
2. Evan Halper, "Shell Adds to Oil Industry's Record Profits, with $41.6 Billion," *Washington Post*, January 31, 2023, https://www.washingtonpost.com/business/2023/01/31/oil-profits-chevron-exxonmobil-earnings/.
3. Of particular interest here are the arguments of Saidiya Hartman and Frank B. Wilderson III. Hartman theorizes Black life after the end of the world in "The End of White Supremacy, an American Romance," *Bomb* 152 (June 5, 2020), https://bombmagazine.org/articles/the-end-of-white-supremacy-an-american-romance/; Wilderson theorizes Blackness *as* the end of the world in *Afropessimism* (New York: Liveright, 2020).
4. See Wendy Brown, "Resisting Left Melancholy," *boundary 2* 26, no. 3 (1999): 19–27; and Jodi Dean, *The Communist Horizon* (London: Verso, 2012).
5. Joan Copjec levels this humorous critique in "Sexual Difference," *Political Concepts*, November 3, 2014, https://www.politicalconcepts.org/sexual-difference-joan-copjec/.
6. See Todd McGowan, *Enjoyment Right and Left* (Minneapolis: Sublation Press, 2022), 10.
7. *The Matrix: Resurrections*, directed by Lana Wachowski (Burbank CA: Warner Bros. Pictures, Village Roadshow Pictures, Venus Castina Productions, 2021).
8. Kate Aronoff, Alyssa Battistoni, Daniel Aldana Cohen, and Thea Riofrancos, *A Planet to Win: Why We Need a Green New Deal* (London: Verso, 2019), 171–72.
9. Aronoff et al., *A Planet to Win*, 172.
10. Aronoff et al., *A Planet to Win*, 175.
11. Aronoff et al., *A Planet to Win*, 175.
12. Todd McGowan, *Capitalism and Desire: The Psychic Cost of Free Markets* (New York: Columbia University Press, 2016), 11; see also 36–41.
13. Aronoff et al., *A Planet to Win*, 176.
14. Alenka Zupančič calls the death drive a "construction site" in *What Is Sex?* (Cambridge MA: MIT Press, 2017), 94.

15. Guardian News, "COP26 Is a Failure: Greta Thunberg Rallies Climate Activists in Glasgow," YouTube, November 5, 2021, 2:53, https://www.youtube.com/watch?v=pHLVDlb6rCU.
16. Jacques Lacan, *The Sinthome: The Seminar of Jacques Lacan, Book XXIII*, ed. Jacques-Alain Miller, trans. A. R. Price (Medford MA: Polity Press, 2016).
17. *It's a Wonderful Life*, directed by Frank Capra (New York: Liberty Films, RKO Radio Pictures, 1946).
18. On the politics of the miracle, see Eric L. Santner, "Miracles Happen: Benjamin, Rosenzweig, Freud, and the Matter of the Neighbor," in *The Neighbor: Three Inquiries in Political Theology*, ed. Slavoj Žižek, Eric L. Santner, and Kenneth Reinhard (Chicago: University of Chicago Press, 2013), 76–133.

IN THE PROVOCATIONS SERIES

Who Would You Kill to Save the World?
Claire Colebrook

Hatred of Sex
Oliver Davis and Tim Dean

Declarations of Dependence: Money, Aesthetics, and the Politics of Care
Scott Ferguson

The People Are Missing: Minor Literature Today
Gregg Lambert

I'm Not Like Everybody Else: Biopolitics, Neoliberalism, and American Popular Music
Jeffrey T. Nealon

Abolishing Freedom: A Plea for a Contemporary Use of Fatalism
Frank Ruda

Dirty Knowledge: Academic Freedom in the Age of Neoliberalism
Julia Schleck

The Earth Is Evil
Steven Swarbrick

Contra Instrumentalism: A Translation Polemic
Lawrence Venuti

Free Listening
Naomi Waltham-Smith

To order or obtain more information on these or other University of Nebraska Press titles, visit nebraskapress.unl.edu.

www.ingramcontent.com/pod-product-compliance
Lightning Source LLC
Chambersburg PA
CBHW030115170426
43198CB00009B/633